*short trips and trails*
# THE COLUMBIA GORGE

*Text: Oral Bullard*
*Photos and Maps: Don Lowe*

**The Touchstone Press**
***P.O. Box 81***
***Beaverton, Oregon 97005***

*Library of Congress*
*Catalog Card No. 73-80049*

*I.S.B.N. No. 0-911518-01-0*

*Copyright © 1974*
*Oral Bullard & Don Lowe*

**Area Map**

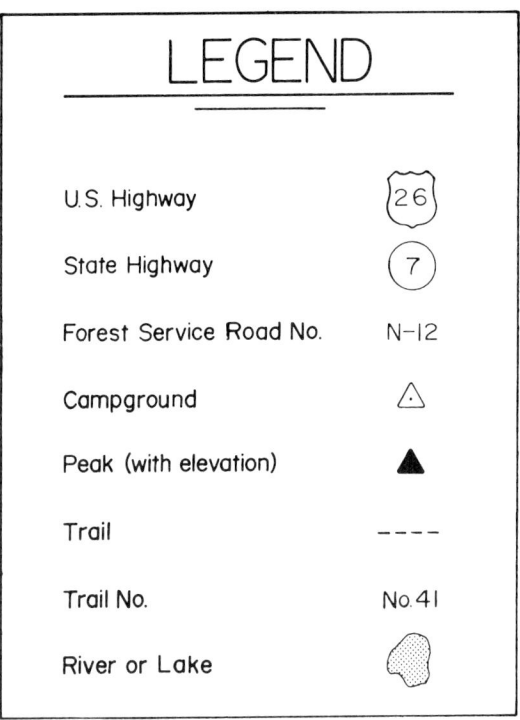

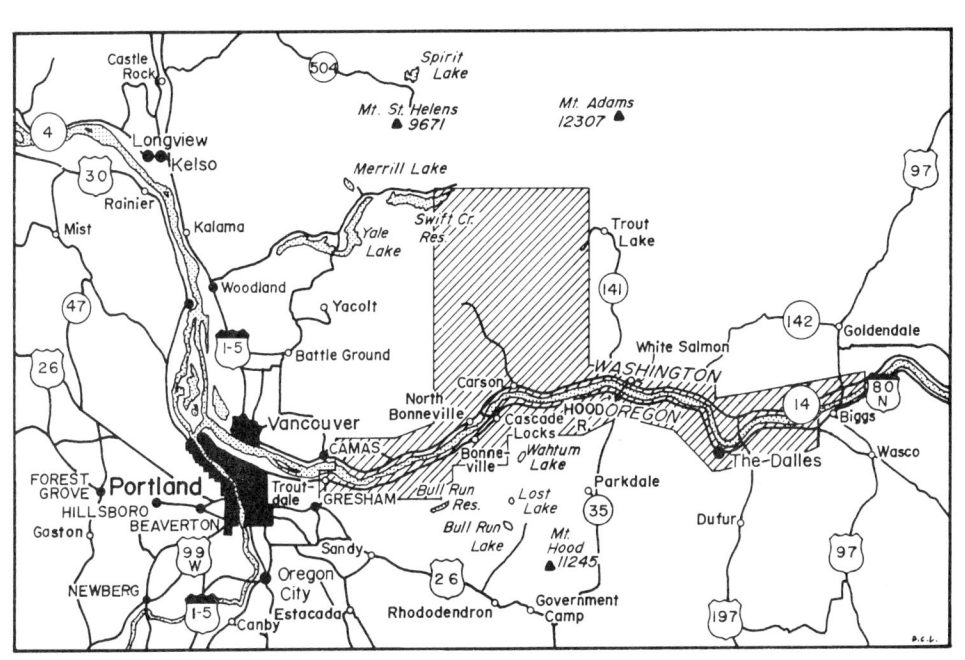

The Columbia River Gorge, from Women's Forum Park.

# contents

| | |
|---|---|
| Discovering the Gorge | 8 |
| The Oregon Experience | 18 |
| Trip 1 • The Old Highway | 27 |
|     Latourell Falls Trail | 36 |
|     Angels Rest Trail | 38 |
|     Wahkeena Falls Trail | 40 |
|     Wahkeena Falls-Multnomah Falls Loop via Perdition Trail | 42 |
|     Multnomah Falls Trail | 44 |
|     Triple Falls Trail | 46 |
|     Horsetail Falls-Oneonta Loop | 47 |
| Trip 1 • Larch Mountain | 48 |
|     Larch Mountain Trail | 48 |
| Trip 3 • Interstate Highway 80-N to Cascade Locks | 53 |
|     McCord Creek Trail | 58 |
|     Tanner Creek Falls Trail | 58 |
|     Wauna Viewpoint Trail | 63 |
|     Eagle Creek Trail | 64 |
|     Buck Point Trail | 66 |
|     Ruckel Creek Trail | 68 |
| Trip 4 • Cascade Locks to Deschutes River | 74 |
|     Herman Creek Loop Trail | 82 |
|     Herman Creek Trail | 83 |
|     Hole-in-the-Walls Fall Trail | 85 |
|     Perham Creek-Wygant Trail | 87 |
| The Washington Experience | 90 |
| Trip 5 • The North Shore | 98 |
|     Beacon Rock Trail | 104 |
|     Rodney Falls-Hardy Falls Trail | 106 |
| Trip 6 • Wind River Loop | 109 |
|     Race Track Trail | 110 |
|     Thomas Lake Trail | 112 |
|     McClellan Meadows Trail | 114 |
|     Lost Lake Trail | 115 |
|     Observation Peak Trail | 116 |
|     Falls Creek Trail | 117 |
| Trip 7 • Big Lava Bed Loop | 121 |
|     Goose Lake Lakeshore Trail | 124 |
|     Big Huckleberry Trail | 124 |
|     Grassy Knoll Trail | 125 |
|     Little Huckleberry Trail | 127 |

**Fisherman on Sandy River.**

# DISCOVERING THE GORGE

Any attempt to describe the Columbia River Gorge with words is doomed to failure. Similarly, even the photographs of one so capable as Don Lowe, my compatriot in this venture, can only hint at the remarkable experience that awaits anyone who ventures up the myriad canyons and along the many trails on either side of the Gorge.

This book is an attempt to encourage such ventures. For those who believe that increased traffic on the Gorge trails invites destruction I can only counter with the belief that increased knowledge and appreciation of the unique aspects of the Gorge may lead to its preservation.

This, then, is an invitation to discovery; a guide to lead you into an experience with more depth than either the words or pictures in this little volume can convey; an attempt to get you out of your car and some short distance from the traffic pounding along the highway.

To truly appreciate the Gorge you must walk, up the trails alongside tumbling waterfalls and rushing streams, to the sylvan beauty of upper Multnomah Creek or along the gentle path to Thomas Lake. How else can you feel the exhilaration of the wind or steep in the view from Angels Rest, or marvel at the strange absence of all sounds except Nature's own in the deep woods along the Herman Creek Trail? To admire the view from the top of Beacon Rock you must first climb it.

The walks described in this book are suitable for entire families. Many of the trails can be walked safely by children no more than 3 or 4 years old. Where there is danger for the very young, that has been noted.

The city or suburban reared youngster will have a grand time along the trail. Alert young eyes will see things of interest that may be lost from a slightly higher eye level or the more jaded viewpoint of the adult, and the questions that come forth from young lips may stir old memories or a desire to learn more about the beauty that

**Hikers pass beneath overhanging cliff at Upper Horsetail Falls.**

surrounds you.

All in all, a walk in the Gorge is a rewarding experience, and later, when you find you are incapable of relating that experience to others, you will know that you have captured, and been captured by, the special spirit that exists in its ravines and forests.

You do not have to qualify as a mountain climber or even a serious advocate of physical fitness to be able to walk for at least some distance along the trails described in this book. You may puff a bit at times, and if that is the case then do not be ashamed to pause and rest a moment to catch your breath before continuing on your way. Besides — what better way is there to study your environment?

The approximate length of each trail is stated and reference to the degree of difficulty is made in the text, so if you are badly out of condition it would be wise to start on the more gentle paths and gradually work your way through those of greater rise and length. If you do these walks on a fairly regular schedule you will find that your conditioning improves rapidly and that those rises flatten out as the muscle tone in your legs improves.

A few suggestions may increase your enjoyment:

You will need adequate clothing. Remember, the sun sets early in many parts of the Gorge and it can chill quite rapidly, even in summer. Judge the amount and kind of clothing you wear by the time of day you begin your walk and the amount of time you plan to spend on the trail. If the trailhead is in open country, with the sun beating down, remember also that the trail may lead you into deep woods, with a resulting drop in temperature. If you decide to do your walking in the fall, winter or spring, light rainwear over a warm jacket is advisable. The simplest rule of thumb is to have more clothing than you think you might need.

As to footwear: I did all of the hikes in this book wearing a pair of relatively inexpensive "waffle-stomper" boots. Thick-soled tennis or deck-type shoes

A curving walkway leads from the Old Highway down to mid-point of the falls at Shepperd's Dell.

would be adequate for most of the walks, but there are rocky portions on many trails, so a good walking shoe or hiking boot is recommended.

Since not all of the trails follow streams, it is best to decide in advance whether or not you will require a canteen of water for your trip. Availability of water is mentioned in the text.

A backpack to carry a few snacks will add enjoyment when you pause to rest or enjoy the view.

Littering is a cardinal sin, but you may see some evidence that your predecessors on the trail have committed it. In that case, you can add to the pleasure of those who will follow by picking up the bit of paper or the discarded container and packing it out to deposit in the nearest trash barrel.

"Stay on the trail" is perhaps the best advice that can be offered. Straying away from the established trail can be extremely dangerous. The woods may be lovely, and the temptation overwhelming, but search parties are called out periodically to locate those who followed temptation and were lost. Rescue parties are sent in for those foolish individuals who edged off the trail "to get a better look" and ended up at the bottom of a cliff or a steep embankment.

"Cutting the switchbacks" is the terminology for taking shortcuts in climbing up to the next trail level. This can be dangerous if you send loose rocks crashing down on persons below you. It also breaks down the established trail, increasing maintenance costs, and is very damaging to the fragile environment of the Gorge.

And, finally, observance of the rules of simple courtesy, such as leaving noise-making transistor radios at home, avoiding exuberant shrieks, and not destroying the trees, shrubs and flowers, not only will make your own journey more pleasant but will add to the enjoyment of others.

If you walk quietly, in safety and in comfort, you will increase your pleasure. Take time to look around you. Listen. The eyes and ears of city-folk are not accustomed to Nature, but you will find that she

**Basaltic cliffs tower majestically over Ainsworth State Park.**

has her own billboards — that flash of color through the trees; a sudden, breathless view; the scurrying feet of a tiny animal; the moss covered trees and boulders, the ferns.

You *can* find solitude in the Gorge, particularly if you avoid the more heavily traveled trails and the summer weekends. The best time to walk in the woods is in the fall or the spring of the year. Even on weekends it is not usually crowded then and the changing of the seasons is an exciting time.

Some years it is possible to take the trails at the lower elevations for the full twelve months, but even in a year with a hard winter most Gorge trails are open from the first of April into November.

Some persons avoid the Gorge in the spring and fall because of the mist, but do not let it deter you. The Gorge mist is part of its magic, and I have covered many miles on dark and gloomy days with the mist against my face and the ragged bits of clouds floating along the ridges above. To be in the Gorge on such a day is to be in communion with it — with the earth, the sky, the water.

The trails do not lack variety. The simple fact of geography insures a wide selection, and for the purposes of definition we have described and photographed areas from the Sandy River, east of Portland, to the Deschutes River on the Oregon side, and from the Skamania County line (23 miles east of Vancouver) east to Stonehenge on the Washington side. Thus one travels (west to east) from the cool, moist climate west of the Cascade Range to the semi-arid region approaching the central deserts.

In addition, a minute portion of the southern Washington Cascades is presented in the area immediately adjacent to two tributaries of the Columbia, the Wind River and the Little White Salmon River. These trips afford a different kind of scenery and experience.

The book is divided into seven specific trip sections, each one involving less than a one day's drive from Portland or Vancouver. On the Oregon side the distances

**Mist Falls cascades down cliff just west of Benson State Park. On a windy day the water is blown away in a fine spray.**

are measured from the generally accepted western terminus of the Gorge, the Sandy River. In Washington no such clear definition exists, so the highway distances are measured from the Interstate Bridge across the Columbia River.

You will find a listing of points of interest, campgrounds, and picnic grounds in each section. Following each trip description is a detailed report of the trails in that section.

Some duplication exists: for instance, Trip No. 4 is an extension of Trip No. 3, but it is virtually impossible to travel even the same route through the Gorge without discovering something new and exciting.

The traveler who races up and down the freeway misses much that is beautiful and inspiring, and, unless he has some knowledge of the area's history, he also fails to appreciate it fully. Thus, brief mention of some of the historical aspects of those things that remain to be seen is included in the text, although this is not intended, in any sense, to be an historical work.

If the Columbia River Gorge and adjacent territory is to be preserved for the generations which follow us it will be because we see it as it is today and decide that it is still worth saving. So take time to look at it as you drive through, and then take the additional time to explore beyond the paved roads, to wander a mile or two into the gentle wilderness, to be calmed by its spirit, enthralled by its beauty.

A walk in the woods is more than an escape from the pressure cooker of modern society, from the speed, frenzy and noise which surrounds us daily. It can be a personal act of faith, a restatement in the belief of the eternity of Nature, which gave birth to all and which will continue to exist long after we are gone.

It can be a moment of freedom, to be remembered and treasured, and beyond that can lead to a re-evaluation of personal priorities and a greater appreciation of all of life itself.

**Below Crown Point the Old Highway winds its way through lush undergrowth and towering conifers.**

# THE OREGON EXPERIENCE

Far too many people regard a tour of the Columbia Gorge as consisting of a stop at Crown Point, another stop at Multnomah Falls, and a quick look at Bonneville Dam.

Then it's back to Portland for the cocktail hour and dinner or else a fast trip east on the freeway.

Such cursory examinations, reminiscent of the touristy "this is Tuesday so it must be Belgium" approach, can be faulted on three counts. First, the stops as listed are the ones most likely to attract crowds. Secondly, they are not, necessarily, either the most interesting or the most impressive points of interest and, finally, any real examination of the Gorge requires a more relaxed approach.

The Columbia River Gorge, unlike a skyscraper or other man-made spectaculars, was not created in a year or even a thousand years. So a proper approach to it requires a sense of history, at the very least a realization that this did not come slap dash off the drawing board but is a creation of Nature over a period beyond man's concept of time.

Historians can tell us when the pyramids were built, or the Colosseum in Rome — but history does not record when the Gorge began for its origin recedes into antiquity, long before man himself.

One of the truly amazing facts about the Gorge is that history beyond the relatively brief span of the last 200 years comes only from the romantic Indian legends or from facts uncovered by geologists. There is some concurrence in legend and fact, but neither of them has yet fixed a date in time and probably they never will.

So, many of the details of the creation of the Gorge will remain forever a mystery and perhaps that is just as well. The human thirst for full knowledge, the urge to know all things, must recognize that some mysteries may never be unraveled.

In recent years we have seen destruction of natural aspects of the Gorge, such as the blocking off of the Cascades, and the

Shepperd's Dell.

drowning of Celilo Falls. "Progress," until recently our most important product, dictated that these changes be made. Progress, and convenience, also dictated that the 80-N Freeway be constructed to hurry us past the scenery.

Yet, overall, the Gorge has changed remarkably little in those 200 years. The trucks that rumble along the freeway may distract you as you hike up to Wauna Point, but the basaltic cliffs remain much as they were then, undefiled. And it is those cliffs which are so much a part of the Oregon experience.

In the winter and spring literally hundreds of waterfalls hang from them like silvery threads, fed by the rain or the melting snow. And although the brooding, tree-covered slopes and bare cliffs may seem impenetrable, the major creeks find openings and plunge through them to mingle their waters with the mighty Columbia itself.

The walker who decides to explore these falls is in for an exciting adventure. First, the rather steep but relatively short trip to the top. Beyond that, a rare beauty that is impossible to describe.

The last major waterfall in the Gorge is Starvation Creek. From there eastward the experience changes as the foliage gradually disappears from the hills and the hills themselves fade back from the roadway.

From Rowena Crest one sees a different kind of beauty, and a feeling of awe that this mighty river was able to carve its way through these barren hills.

Many of the old landmarks are gone. Celilo Falls was once the great fishing spot and trade center for the Indians, who came from as far away as the Rocky Mountains to barter. The Dalles Dam eliminated Celilo Falls.

The Dalles was where "the river turned sideways" and rushed through a crevass in a raging torrent. The Cascades were rapids that were obliterated by Bonneville Dam.

Other landmarks were only partially obscured. In the center of the river the tip of Memaloose, "The Island of the Dead," still is visible above the impounded waters.

A drive west through the Gorge in the

One section of the Old Military Road still intact on Shellrock Mountain.

late afternoon is another interesting way to capture the Oregon experience.

From Celilo Park the lowering sun reflects off the great expanse of water and suddenly you round a turn and, with marvelous clarity, you are head-on with Mount Hood.

As the foliage on the hills thickens beyond Hood River, the clouds roll in from the Pacific and the hills, clear cut against the sky but moments before, are shrouded in mist. Below Bonneville Dam the river is free at last for the final run to the sea.

To the left, now, St. Peters Dome, the cathedral-shaped rock that man named after a distant place of worship, stands out against the cliffs behind Ainsworth State Park. Farther on is the mighty plunge of Multnomah Falls and just beyond that, high on the cliff, Mist Falls is blown into a fine spray by the wind.

Also high up to your left the Vista House at Crown Point is reminiscent of some ancient castle while to your right, at the river's edge, is Rooster Rock.

Other sights you may have missed along the way include the delicate spray of "Lancaster Falls" just west of Starvation Creek; the brief glimpse of the remnants of the old Military Road on Shellrock Mountain. If you raced by the town of Cascade Locks without stopping then you did not see that section of the old canal, where fishermen back up their campers, set out their lines, and retire in comfort for a beer or a cup of coffee.

You may make this trip a dozen times and find something new in every journey.

The Oregon experience is a blend of Nature and of man, a mixture of natural beauty and poetic thought. The hills and cliffs, bleached by the sun in the east, softened by the bounty of rain in the west, are a work of art, a loving handicraft of creation that man could not duplicate, not even given the millions of years that it has already existed.

**Dramatic contrasts highlight The Oregon Experience. Lone walker and dog stroll on sand dunes near Columbia River east of The Dalles while (overleaf) dense fog blankets the Sandy River Valley.**

# Trips 1 and 2

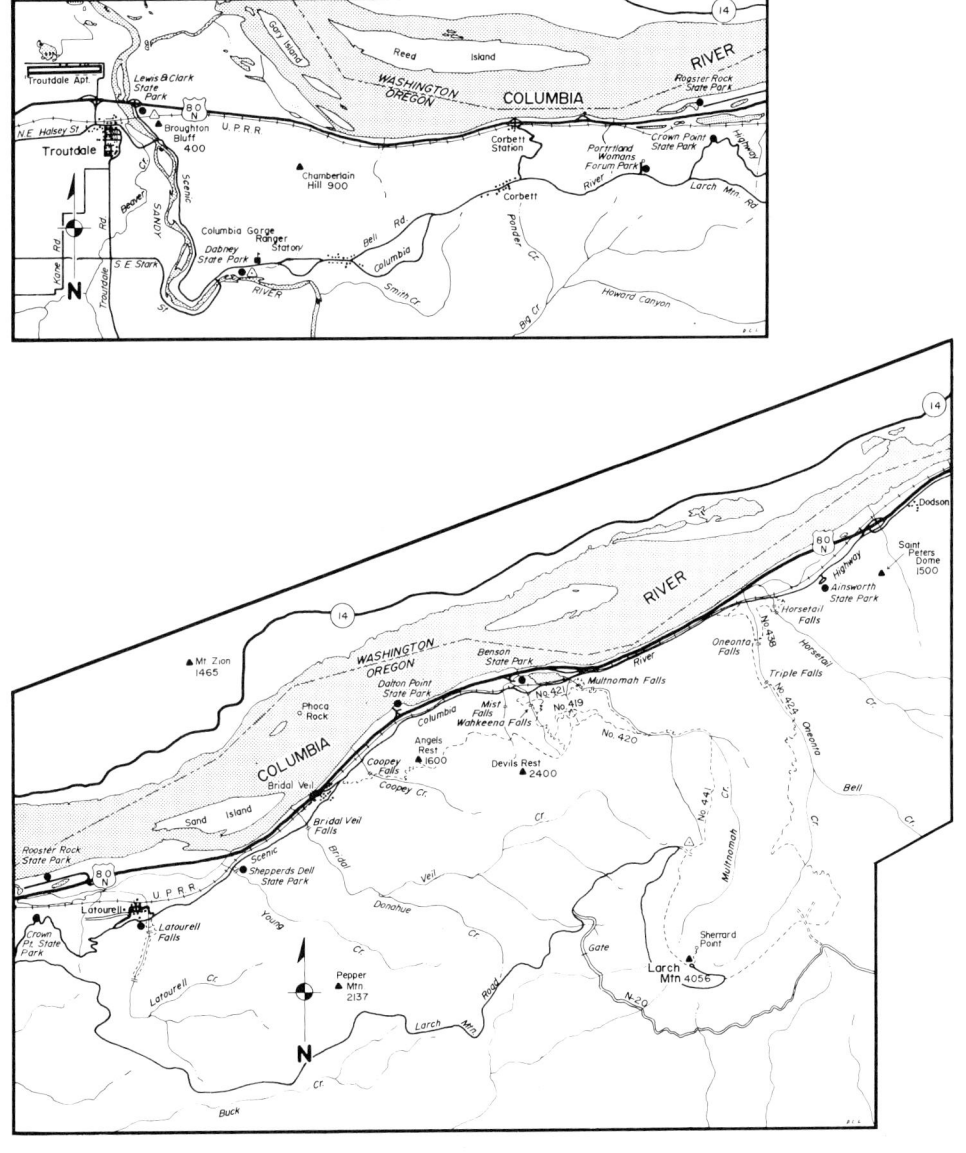

## Trip 1 • The Old Highway

**Points of Interest:** Women's Park at Chanticleer Point, Vista House at Crown Point, Shepperd's Dell, Lookout at Latourell Falls, Wahkeena Falls, Multnomah Falls and Lodge, Oneonta Gorge, Horsetail Falls.

**Picnic Grounds:** Lewis & Clark State Park, Guy W. Talbot State Park, Wahkeena Falls Picnic area, J. C. Ainsworth State Park Picnic area.

**Camp Grounds:** Dabney State Park, J. C. Ainsworth State Park.

**Trails:** Latourell Falls, Angels Rest, Wahkeena Falls, Wahkeena Falls-Multnomah Falls Loop, Upper Multnomah Falls, Triple Falls, Horsetail Falls-Oneonta Gorge Loop.

The Columbia River Highway, dedicated on June 7, 1916, was called "a poem in stone." Brief sections of it still exist today and are a memorial to the many men who built it.

The longest section still extant now is called "The Scenic Highway," which winds and twists for approximately 12 miles through some of the most spectacular scenery in the Gorge. It is heavily traveled in summer and you will find yourself proceeding at a leisurely pace, so take time to enjoy the scenery and also the bits of the lovely old stone walls.

Samuel Christopher Lancaster, the consulting engineer when the highway was built, said of these walls: "Dry masonry walls (constructed without the use of cement or mortar of any kind) have been used extensively in Germany, Italy, Switzerland and Greece in bygone centuries.

"We adopted this plan and constructed many miles of dry masonry walls on the steep slopes of the mountains of the Columbia Gorge. They add greatly to the charm of the highway.

"The Italian laborers built their very souls into these walls as they sang their native songs and thought of the homeland."

**Moss covers section of stone wall along the Old Highway.**

To reach this road, drive east of Portland on Interstate Highway 80-N to the Sandy River. (You will see "Scenic Highway" turn-off signs prior to reaching the Sandy, but I personally prefer the route described below.)

Take the Lewis & Clark State Park exit immediately east of the Sandy River. Turn left after the exit and proceed along the east side of the Sandy.

As you follow the river you will pass through an area of homes on the right and a steep bank to your left. At 2.4 miles from the freeway exit you will come to the entrance to Dabney State Park where you will find campsites and a good beach.

Proceed along the highway, following "Scenic Highway" signs, and the road soon begins to climb away from the Sandy River. At 3.5 miles you enter the village of Springdale. The road continues to climb to the town of Corbett (6.0 miles).

Just past Corbett you will begin to see the mountains on the Washington side of the Columbia River. The Portland Women's Forum Park at Chanticleer Point (8.0 miles), affords the first real vista up the Columbia and is an excellent spot from which to take photographs. Straight ahead you will see the Vista house at Crown Point.

Half a mile farther on the road splits, the right fork leading to the top of Larch Mountain. Follow the road straight ahead, and almost at once you will begin to see portions of the old stone masonry.

At the Vista House you will get a marvelous view upriver, as well as a glimpse of Rooster Rock below. The Vista House was built in 1917 and the highway loops immediately below it were considered an engineering masterpiece. A plaque on the building honors Samuel C. Lancaster, 1864-1941, and reads: "Chief Engineer Scenic Columbia River Highway, 1913-15. Pioneer builder of hard surface roads. His genius overcame tremendous obstacles, extending and replacing a highway of poetry and drama so that millions could enjoy God's spectacular creations."

The Vista House contains a gift shop and restrooms.

**Dabney State Park on the Sandy River has picnic area, overnight facilities, sandy beaches.**

From Crown Point the road loops down towards the Columbia River. At 11.5 miles you will come to the entrance to Guy W. Talbot State Park, which has picnic facilities and parking spaces for 30 cars.

The first of the major Gorge waterfalls is Latourell (12.0 miles). Park just after you cross the old bridge, and do take the time to walk the 200 feet to the view point.

Shepperd's Dell, the second waterfall, is just slightly more than a mile beyond Latourell. A lovely little walkway leads down to the mid-point of the falls. Again, park just after you cross the bridge. This is an ideal spot for photography, either from the road or from the walkway.

You will cross the bridge at the head of Bridal Veil Falls, but there is no good view of it on this particular route. The hamlet of Bridal Veil is just beyond the falls.

Wahkeena is an Indian word meaning "most beautiful." A description most fitting for Wahkeena Falls (17.4 miles). You will find ample parking and a small picnic area to your right, at the base of the falls, as well as a much larger picnic area to your left. A shelter house and toilet facilities are located here.

Multnomah Falls is the most spectacular of all the waterfalls on this trip and easily the most popular tourist spot in this section of the Gorge. Multnomah Falls Lodge contains restrooms, a gift shop, a snack bar in summer, a restaurant, coffee shop, bar, and visitor's center. It was built by the City of Portland in 1925 and donated to the Federal Government in 1943. It is now operated by permit issued by the Forest Service.

Cameras whir and click at Multnomah Falls, but not always from the best vantage points. Take the walk up to the bridge, and look for good camera angles along the way. There is a problem with spray here when attempting to take photos.

Oneonta Gorge (20.3 miles) is a narrow slit in the rocks. Stop here long enough to walk down to the creek level. A friend of mine says that he and his family have played a little game for years, attempting to walk up to the waterfall at the head of Oneonta Gorge without getting their feet

Vista House at Crown Point on cliff high above Interstate 80-N, with Rooster Rock in background along the Columbia River.

wet. At last report, only one member of the family had succeeded.

The water is cold, the rocks are slippery, but there is no danger except for very small children.

Just east of Horsetail Falls, a slight distance beyond Oneonta, there is the first small picnic area which is part of J. C. Ainsworth State Park. Horsetail Falls plunges 176 feet into a circular pool and since it is close to the roadside the mist created by the drop frequently drifts across the road.

The entrance to the camping area at Ainsworth State Park is 21.5 miles from the Sandy River exit. Forty-five campsites are located on two levels. The area has holding tank disposals, large restrooms and showers. A nightly fee is charged.

This is the favored campsite in the Gorge and in the summertime it is frequently filled up from Thursday afternoon through Sunday night, as trailer campers from all over the United States use this as a headquarters while they visit Portland or take trips up and down the Columbia Gorge or to Mount Hood.

Towering cliffs rise directly to the south, and St. Peter's Dome looms majestically over Ainsworth Park. If you are interested in taking a short walk, locate a path leading to the west on the road connecting the two levels of the park. Follow the path for about 200 yards and you will come to a maintenance road. Turn right on the road and follow it down to one of the picnic areas alongside the Scenic Highway.

Another pleasant little walk is the Ainsworth Loop Trail, which is one-half mile long. From the first (most westerly) picnic area at Ainsworth, follow the sign at the west end of the area. The trail loops up above and to the west, then switches back to the east and comes out at the second picnic area.

You have now reached the end of Trip No. 1, for just east of Ainsworth State Park you will re-join the freeway for your return trip to Portland.

You have traveled over a section of one of the most famous highways in the United States; a road that has been compared

**Oneonta Gorge.**

favorably to the Axenstrasse in Switzerland; a highway that Frederick Villiers, correspondent for the Illustrated London News, called "the king of roads."

The Old Highway was a labor of love, a triumph in its own age. On your journey you have not only glimpsed some of the great scenery of the Gorge, you have also driven along the visible remains of the dream of Samuel Hill, who conceived the idea for the road, and Samuel Christopher Lancaster, the remarkable genius who insisted that it be a work of art.

**Unusual winter storm turns the Gorge into an icy wonderland.**

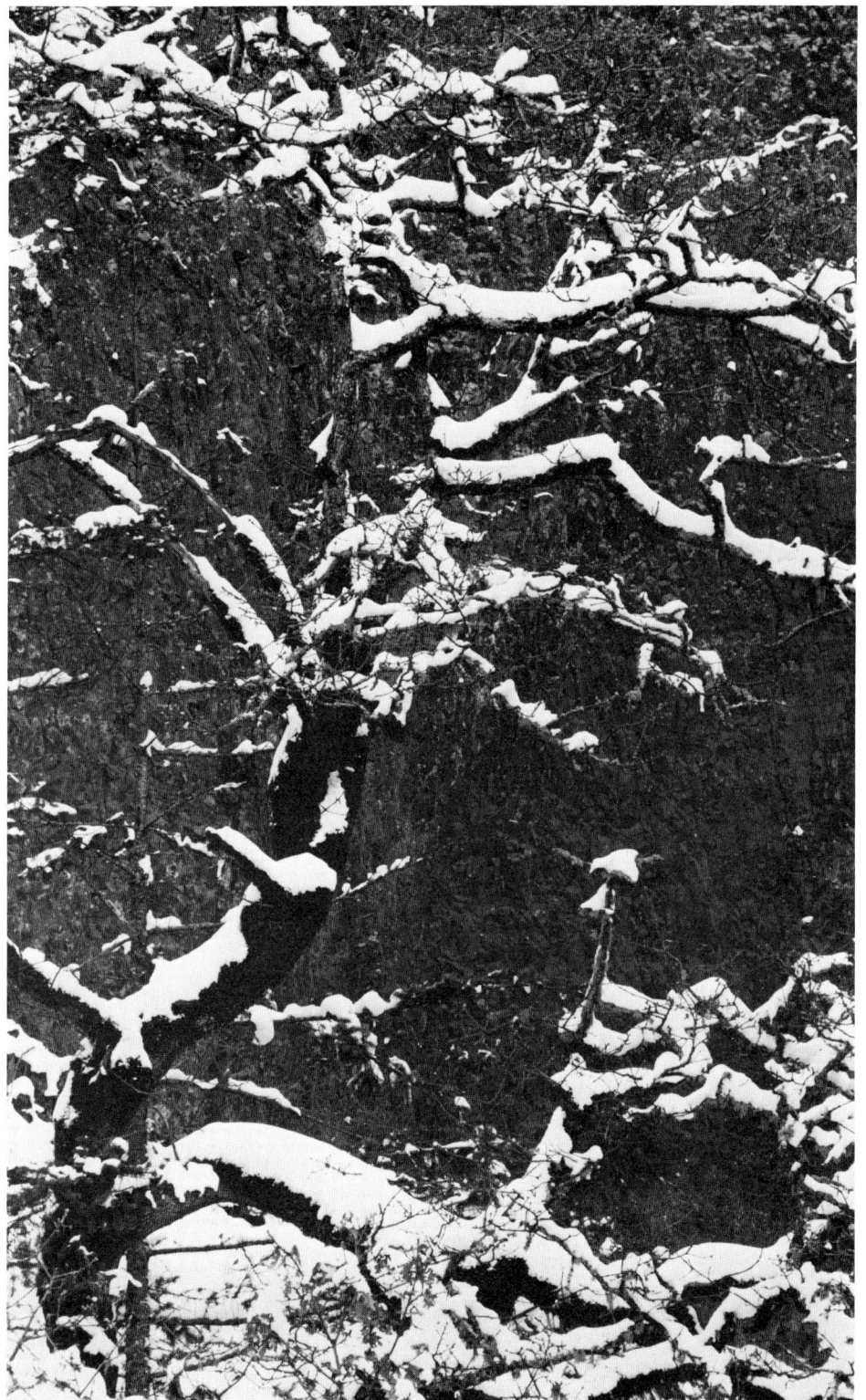

### Trip 1, Trail 1 • Latourell Falls

**Lower Falls Loop approximately 1.0 mile.**
**Upper Falls Loop approximately 2.0 miles**

The Latourell Falls Trail is one of the prettiest walks in the Gorge. There are no dizzying heights and few large trees. It is particularly recommended in either the fall or the spring because of the great number of deciduous trees which are at their most beautiful moments in these seasons.

From the west end of the parking lot east of the bridge on the Old Highway take the lower trail which leads to a footbridge at the base of the falls. Cross the bridge, then follow the path north along the west side of the creek, back under the highway to Guy W. Talbot State Park. From the park follow the sign which reads "Loop Trail" back to the highway west of the bridge to where another sign designates "Loop Trip, Upper Falls."

Cross the highway and climb switchbacks to the top of the ridge. There are no false trails and you simply follow the path down to the footbridge which crosses the creek above the falls.

You are now about one-half mile from the park. If you cross the footbridge and return to the highway you will have completed the Lower Falls Loop. To continue on to the Upper Falls take the path to the right just before you reach the footbridge. This goes along the west bank of the creek for about 300 yards before the switchback takes you higher, but it is a gentle climb to the base of the Upper Falls.

Cross the footbridge here to the east side of the creek and return to the bridge above the Lower Falls. There is a short side trail to viewpoint at the head of the falls; the path then leads back to the parking lot east of the bridge on the Old Highway.

**Latourell Falls is the first of the major waterfalls in the Columbia River Gorge.**

**Trip 1, Trail 2 • Angels Rest**

**Approximate distance: 1.8 miles (1 way)**

This trail is neither marked nor numbered, yet it is easy to locate. Just after you cross the bridge over Bridal Veil Falls, and before you enter the village of Bridal Veil itself, you come to the Bridal Veil Junction. Park your car in the open space where the roads meet and proceed down the Old Highway (towards the town of Bridal Veil) about 100 yards. You will see the path leading up from the south side of the road.

The trip to Angels Rest should be taken on a clear day, because you will enjoy one of the better views to the west from the windswept plateau.

The trail goes up through a canopy of trees in a long switchback. After a few hundred yards the trail crosses a rockslide, then follows the edge of a ridge above Coopey Creek. Just before you get to Coopey Falls the trail splits. Take either trail, for they rejoin shortly.

A log and board bridge spans Coopey Creek above the falls, after which the trail rises to the south on the east side of the creek. Several switchbacks lead through lush undergrowth where trees keep the trail well shaded. Near the top you break out of the trees, and very shortly after that the trail contours around to the south side of Angels Rest, where you cross a slab rock slope.

The crest itself is large and flat and the panoramic view makes it an ideal spot for photography. Follow along the bluff to the north to get the best view.

The trip to Angels Rest is a steady but not exhausting climb. The elevation gain is almost 1,500 feet and although there are no abrupt rises neither are there any level walks to break the climb.

On one of my trips up the trail I met a family of 4 on the crest. The youngest was 6 years old. They told me they had "dawdled along" but had made the one way in less than 3 hours. Without small children the trip can be made in about one-half that time.

**Dense undergrowth of deciduous trees line many trails in the heart of the Gorge.**

## Trip 1, Trail 3 • Wahkeena Falls

### 1.5 miles (1 way) to intersection with Larch Mountain Trail

The trailhead is at the west end of the south parking lot. There is one switchback to the stone bridge at the base of the falls, where the paved trail ends. Take the first switchback to the right at the intersection with Perdition Trail.

On the first part of this trail watch for persons above you as there is a considerable quantity of loose rock that can tumble down. By the same token, be considerate of those below you and stay on the trail to avoid sending rocks down on them.

The Wahkeena Trail rises in short switchbacks directly above the Wahkeena Falls picnic area. At the top a trail leads left to Monument View Point.

A particular section of the total cataract of Wahkeena is known as Necktie Falls. A partially fenced and partially handrailed trail leads to the edge of these falls. Handholding of small children is recommended if you take this short side trip.

The main Wahkeena Falls trail goes to a wooden footbridge about 175 yards farther upstream and from there the trail leads up a narrow canyon beside the tumbling waters of the creek. You will soon cross another bridge to the opposite side.

If you decide to proceed on up the trail above Necktie Falls, *please* go as far as to the point where two creeks meet. Here lacy white water tumbles around moss-covered stones, while new growth rises out of a rotting old log that slants vertically down the center of a small falls.

From this point the trail switches back and forth between the east and west forks of the creek. At one point you will walk under a huge old log and ford a tiny creek — one leap will get you across!

At 1.5 miles the trail intersects with the Larch Mountain Trail. You may return down the Wahkeena Trail, stopping to enjoy the many fine views along the way, or you can take the Larch Mountain Trail down to the Multnomah Falls Lodge parking lot and back to the base of Wahkeena Falls via Return Trail.

Wahkeena — "most beautiful".

**Trip 1, Trail 4 • Wahkeena Falls-Multnomah Falls Loop via Perdition Trail No. 421 and Return Trail No. 442**

**Approximate distance: 3.0 miles (round trip)**

The Perdition Trail connects the Wahkeena Falls Trail and the Upper Multnomah Falls Trail (Larch Mountain). Start out on the Wahkeena Falls Trail and follow it for one-half mile to the Perdition Trail marker. The Perdition Trail parallels the Columbia River for a short distance, then rises up concrete steps (with handrail) and shortly after that turns south and follows the west bank of a tiny brook. After crossing the brook, the trail switches back to a point overlooking the river.

From there a series of wooden steps leads east along the top of the ridge. At the end of the first section of these steps a viewpoint trail goes about 30 yards to overlook Benson Park.

Continue east along the top of the ridge. After a short descent there is another viewpoint trail about 40 yards long to a point where Multnomah Falls is visible straight ahead.

The main trail continues to the right of the viewpoint trail then winds south around a ravine which is crossed at its head by a small footbridge. Shortly after you make that crossing the trail Y's. The left trail goes about 80 yards to a point where there is another view of the top of Multnomah Falls, the trail on the right of the Y follows along the top of a steep embankment, and is partially fenced to protect against the abrupt drop off to the left.

The trail emerges just behind and slightly above Multnomah Falls and continues east along the south side of Multnomah Creek to the intersection with the Larch Mountain Trail. Turn left at the intersection, cross the bridge and follow the trail down to the lodge.

Return Trail No. 441 can be found just west of the lodge parking lot. The Forest Service has difficulty keeping trail markers here, so there may not be one on any particular day, but the path leading off to the left is easy to locate.

*Tree rises from top of rock formation above Perdition Trail. by stone markers.*

*Many Gorge trails are still identified by stone markers (lower right).*

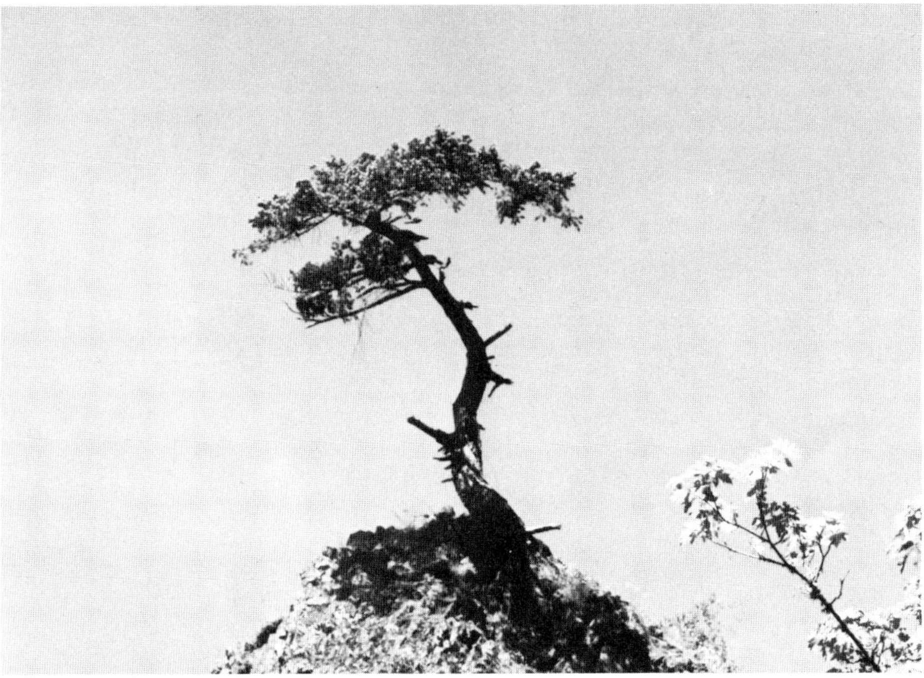

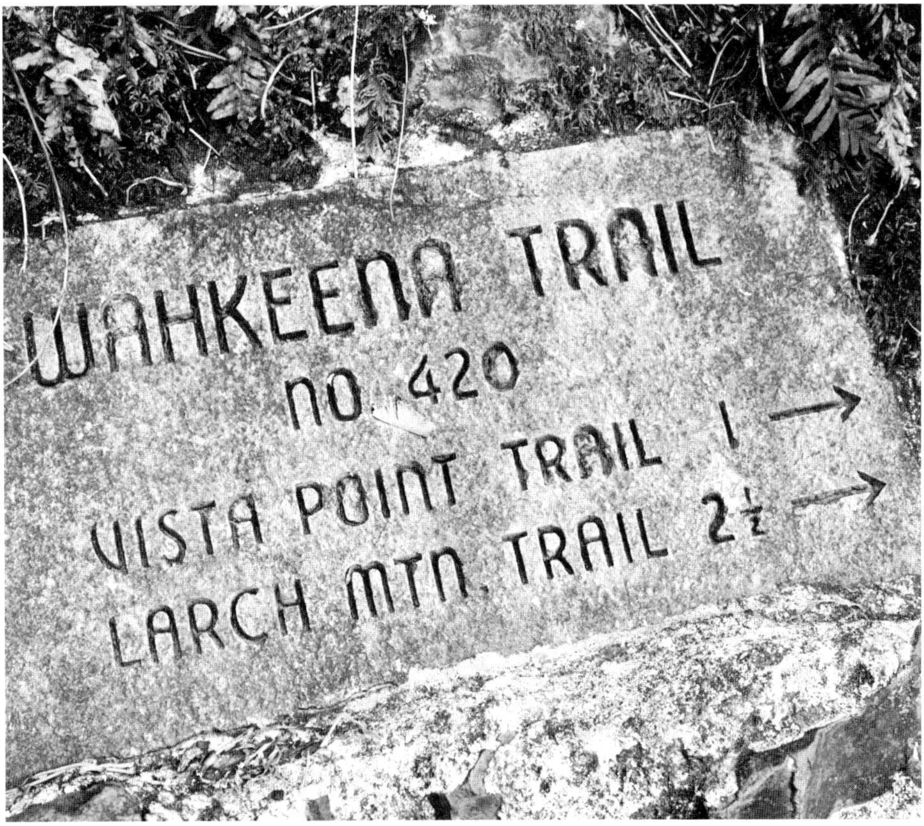
WAHKEENA TRAIL
NO. 420
VISTA POINT TRAIL 1
LARCH MTN. TRAIL 2½

**Trip 1, Trail 5 • Multnomah Falls (Larch Mountain Trail No. 441) to Upper Multnomah Falls**
**Approximate distance: 1.3 miles (1 way)**

Tourists scurry up and down the lower levels of this trail in such great numbers that the Forest Service has now hard surfaced the trail to the top of the ridge.

The majority of those who climb to the top go to the falls viewpoint platform and then return to the lodge parking lot, but the best scenery is to the left on the trail leading to the Upper Falls.

Start from the parking lot, just east of the lodge, and follow the switchbacks to the stone bridge, which is a popular stop. From there you can take the very short side trip down to a pool at the base of the main drop of the falls.

The trail goes east from the bridge and switchbacks lead to the top of the ridge. You will see a sign in the rock indicating the viewpoint trail to the head of the falls. Follow this trail if you enjoy standing on a platform overlooking the lodge.

The Larch Mountain Trail, however, goes east along Multnomah Creek, then crosses it on an intriguing old stone bridge. The trail here intersects with the Perdition Trail (to the right).

Continue on to the left along the Larch Mountain Trail. It is an easy, almost level walk, and the waters of the creek tumble over and around large boulders. Shortly before you reach the upper falls you walk along the base of a cliff at the creek's edge.

You can continue on up the trail, past the upper falls, and find some pleasant scenery, but it is more than 5 miles to the top of Larch Mountain, so if you want to see the area beyond this point it is recommended that you take the Larch Mountain Trail from the top down. (See trip No. 2 for details of that journey.)

*Mighty Multnomah is largest and most spectacular waterfall in the Gorge. There are parking lots along both the Old Highway and Interstate 80-N so tourists may view the falls.*

## Trip 1, Trail 6 • Triple Falls (Oneonta Trail No. 424)

**Approximate distance: 1.5 miles (1 way)**

The trailhead is just two miles east of Multnomah Falls on the Old Highway, and there is parking space in an open area on the north side of the highway across from the small sign which reads, "Oneonta Trail No. 424, Larch Mtn. 8."

Since there is a drop off to the left on portions of this trail precautions should be taken with small children. However, it is neither dangerous nor difficult.

The trail leads up the bank to the southwest, then switches back to the left. After some rise it turns south and continues up the west bank of Oneonta Gorge. At one-half mile the trail intersects with Horsetail Falls Trail No. 438. Keep to the right and proceed on Trail No. 424.

Although the trail climbs well above Oneonta Creek the rises are interspersed with level "breather" stretches. There is only one other set of switchbacks, the first occurring about one-third of a mile from Triple Falls. On the last 100 yards or so to the falls you will find some small switchbacks on the downgrade, and one very short trail off to the left which gives you the best front view of the falls for photographic purposes.

Triple Falls is so named because the creek has cut three definite channels in the rock. The trail crosses the creek just above the falls, and there are round concrete steppingstones to help you get across.

This is one of those idyllic spots, a good place to sit down on a log, munch an apple or a sandwich, and contemplate the natural surroundings, which have been marred only by those artificial stones.

From here you can wander out close to the top of the falls, or continue on up the trail, which parallels the creek for a short distance.

If you have not yet made the Horsetail-Oneonta Loop trip you might want to take the short walk down the Horsetail Falls trail to the bridge over Oneonta Creek on your return.

**Horsetail Falls plunges 176 feet into pool beside the Old Highway.**

## Trip 1, Trail 7 • Horsetail Falls-Oneonta Loop

**Approximate distance: 2.0 miles (round trip)**

The Horsetail Falls-Oneonta Loop trip is one of the three most popular trails in the Gorge (the other two being Eagle Creek and Multnomah Falls). The trail is open usually all year long, since the elevation gain is only about 400 feet. So if you want to avoid crowds, save it for the fall and winter.

The trail, No. 438, starts just east of Horsetail Falls and rises steadily for about one-fifth of a mile, but then is nearly level until the descent at the western end.

It is about one-half mile from the trailhead to the upper falls. Here the trail passes along the cliff beneath the falls, which cascades out over your head into a pool below. The trail then circles around to the right for a short distance before it turns south above the east side of Oneonta Gorge.

At one point there is a little loop trail off to the right that leads out to the top of a cliff overlooking the Columbia River.

As you make the slight descent to the footbridge over the creek, take time to pause at a small lookout to enjoy the view down the narrow fissure through which Oneonta Creek passes. Important: stay on the trail to avoid dangerous cliffs.

The bridge affords another excellent view of Oneonta Gorge. From the bridge the trail rises up the west bank and joins Oneonta Trail No. 424. Take the trail to the right and enjoy the walk back to the Old Highway.

At the point where you start the descent to the highway, a trail leads off to the right to the top of a cliff overlooking the Columbia River. The main trail is to the left. Near the end, follow the right fork of the trail, as the left fork brings you out on the Old Highway at a point where it is quite narrow. The right fork leads down to a point just west of Oneonta Gorge and from there it is a walk of one-half mile along the highway back to Horsetail Falls.

**Walkers pause on bridge over creek above Oneonta Gorge.**

# Trip 2 • Larch Mountain

**Point of interest:** Sherrard Point.
**Picnic area:** Top of Larch Mountain.
**Trail:** Larch Mountain Trail No. 441.

In a year of normal moisture the trail from the top of Larch Mountain can be walked May through October, and some winters it is open for even longer periods.

Two cars are required to accomplish the one-way walk down Larch Mountain. Park one at Multnomah Falls, then drive the other toward Portland on Interstate 80-N to the Corbett exit.

Proceed up Corbett Hill road for 1.8 miles, and take the Crown Point exit at the top of the hill, then turn left on the Old Highway for approximately 2.0 miles to Larch Mountain Road. (For those who do not intend to walk down, follow the directions in trip No. 1 and exit to the Larch Mountain Road where indicated.) It is approximately 14.0 miles from the exit road to the Larch Mountain parking lot.

A large picnic area and flush toilets are available near the parking area. Sherrard Point can be reached on Trail No. 443 from the northeast end of the parking lot. It is a hard-surfaced trail, about 400 yards long, and involves climbing stairs to the concrete platform from which, on a clear day, you can see Mt. Rainier and Mt. St. Helens in Washington as well as Mt. Hood and Mt. Jefferson in Oregon.

## Trip 2, Trail 1 • Larch Mountain Trail No. 441

### Distance: 7.0 miles (1 way)

If you want to enjoy the unique experience of walking down a mountain that you have not climbed, Larch Mountain is the place.

But remember one very special rule for this walk: carry the keys to that car you left at Multnomah Falls!

There is another suggestion, albeit unromantic — be sure your toenails are trimmed short. Misery is sore feet and long toenails pushing continually against the front of your shoe on the downgrade will

**Mount Hood from Larch Mountain.**

guarantee a foot problem before you reach the level ground at the bottom of the trail.

Also, the trail is quite rocky in spots so be sure you wear shoes with heavy soles. Downhill walking does involve some special consideration for your feet, although it is admittedly easier on your heart, lungs and legs.

The trailhead is at the southwest corner of the parking lot and is clearly marked. The trail skirts the picnic area for a short distance, then proceeds through the woods on a gentle downgrade for 1.5 miles, where it is intersected by a service road.

After that the trail becomes somewhat rockier, the downgrade slightly steeper. You will interesect with Multnomah Creek Way at 2.0 miles and just about halfway down you will cross the tiny stream you have been hearing for the last mile or so. The trail follows this stream for another one-half mile then crosses another brook.

The rest of the trip to the top of Multnomah Falls you will be paralleling the creek, sometimes near water level, sometimes a distance above it. If you have small children it is best to keep them within eyesight.

At one point you will see there is both a "Low Water Trail" and a "High Water Trail." The low water trail is passable virtually all of the summer and fall months.

The creek continues to increase in size as many small streams join it and the trail finally crosses a bridge to the west side of the creek. About 150 yards past this bridge the trail Y's at the intersection with the Wahkeena Trail No. 420 (See Trip 1, Trail 3). Take the trail to the right and very shortly you will be at the top of the first of two upper falls on Multnomah Creek.

There is a drop to the right here, so again, keep your eye on any small children you have with you. The trail winds down to the creek level, affording a view of the lower of the two falls.

The intersection with Perdition Trail is approximately one-third of a mile farther on, after a delightful walk along Multnomah Creek. Turn right at the Perdition Trail intersection and cross the stone

**Along the Larch Mountain Trail.**

bridge. After a short climb up the opposite bank you will wind down to the lodge and the parking lot at the base of Multnomah Falls.

Even at a leisurely pace, you can walk this trail in 3.5 hours, including a lunch stop. The scenery becomes progressively more interesting as you descend, a definite plus factor if you begin to tire. Aside from the scenery, the trail offers one-half day of peace and quiet — a rare commodity.

## Trip 3

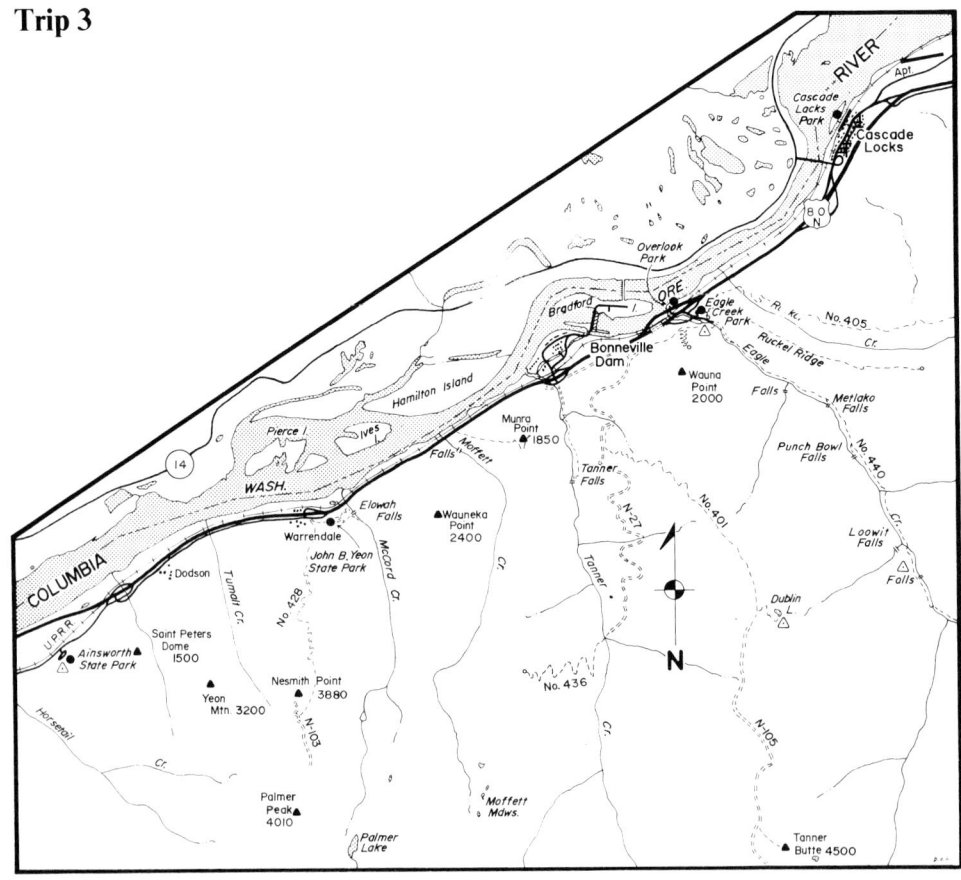

# Trip 3 • Interstate Highway 80-N from the Sandy River to Cascade Locks

**Points of interest:** Rooster Rock, Mist Falls, Multnomah Falls, Bonneville Dam, Oregon State Fish Hatchery, Eagle Creek and Shady Glen Trail, Bridge of the Gods, Cascade Locks, Moffett Creek Arch.

**Picnic grounds:** Rooster Rock State Park (also beach and boat launch), Benson State Park, Eagle Creek, Overlook picnic area at Eagle Creek, Cascade Locks City Park.

**Campgrounds:** Forest Service Campground at Eagle Creek.

**Trails:** McCord Creek (upper and lower falls), Tanner Creek, Eagle Creek, Wauna Viewpoint, Buck Point, Ruckel Creek.

Most travelers on Interstate 80-N hurtle along at maximum speeds and thus get only occasional glimpses of the scenery.

While you can't dawdle along the freeway you CAN turn off occasionally to explore. This trip assumes you are travelling east.

At 5.5 miles after you cross the Sandy River you will get a good view of the Vista House at Crown Point (up and to your right) and Rooster Rock, along the river to your left.

One amusing story about how the name "Rooster Rock" came into being, is that young Indians used the vicinity for a trysting place, so the early white settlers gave it a rather blunt descriptive name which cartographers later changed for the ladies of a more genteel age.

Whatever the origin of its name, it is an interesting obelisk. You pass directly by it at 6.6 miles, and reach the entrance to Rooster Rock State Park at just past 7.0 miles. No overnight facilities are available, but on a summer week-end, when the Columbia is low, the wide, sandy beach is crowded with picnickers and sunbathers. Ample parking, restrooms, and a boat ramp will be found here.

At approximately 10.5 miles look to your right for Bridal Veil Falls, and after another 3.0 miles you will come to the exit road to Benson State Park.

A good view of Wahkeena Falls is obtained from the park and to its right (west) is Mist Falls, where the water falls free from a cliff and on a windy day is literally blown away in a fine cloud of spray.

Benson Park has parking spaces for approximately 200 cars, restrooms and stoves, but no overnight facilities.

From this point on the freeway you can also get a clear view of Beacon Rock, on the Washington state side of the river.

Multnomah Falls exit road is 14.0 miles from the Sandy, with lots of parking spaces just off the freeway and a walkway under the road to the lodge.

Horsetail Falls is also visible from the freeway. At 19.2 miles you reach the exit road to Ainsworth State Park. (Exit here if you wish to visit Yeon State Park and walk up to McCord Creek Falls.)

The freeway passes over both McCord Creek and Moffett Creek before the exit to Bonneville Dam and the Oregon State Fish Hatchery (23.1 miles).

Construction on Bonneville Dam was begun in 1933, and completed in 1939. The impounded waters innundated the Cascades (rapids) in the Columbia River and made large scale upriver barge travel feasible.

You can watch the salmon and other fish going upstream via the fish ladders at Bonneville Dam. A gift shop and restrooms are located above the fish ladders.

As you drive back to the freeway, stop at the Oregon State Fish Hatchery, which features a trout pool and a sturgeon pool. A visit to the holding pens, where the adult salmon are stripped of their eggs, is not particularly recommended as a spawning fish is not a thing of beauty. Better to remember the salmon as king of the river!

However, do take the time to walk along the edge of the hatchery, where hundreds of thousands of salmon fingerlings darken the water, and visit the buildings where you will learn something about the history of fish.

Just east on the freeway from the Bonneville exit you will pass through a tunnel

**Waterfall along the Tanner Creek Trail.**

and as you emerge from it the Eagle Creek exit is to your right.

Anther fish hatchery is located here, and a Forest Service campground is behind and above it.

Park in the picnic area and walk across the suspension bridge to the Shady Glen Trail. This is a short nature trail, and many small signs identify the flora of the area. Good education for the children – and adults, too.

Another interesting side trip is to the Overlook picnic area. This is north across (actually under) the freeway. Although use of the Overlook area may be limited to groups, take a moment to visit it if it is open to the public. A winding trail leads up the knoll from the north end of the parking lot and then switches back to bring you alongside a lovely stone fence at the top. Follow the fence along the west and north brow of the hill to a unique shelter house that was originally intended to contain specimens and photos of some of the local history. The Eagle Creek area is noted for its ancient flora specimens, unearthed in the early 1900's from ancient fossil beds.

Follow along the fence to the steps that lead down to a path to the river's edge. A fence along the water prevents access to the river, but this is a particularly enchanting spot in the summertime when most of the noise of the freeway is drowned out by the wind in the trees and bird songs.

Exit from the freeway at 26.5 miles to Cascade Locks. The town itself makes an interesting side trip, with excellent photographic possibilities along the old canal and a great deal of historical interest. The old museum is a delight.

If the tramway project now under consideration is authorized the unique flavor of this little city will inevitably undergo some change. It is an historical spot, due to the old canal, and worthy of some of your time. (Plans call for the tramway base to be south of the Bridge of the Gods and the tramway will rise to one of the ridges high above the city.)

From Cascade Locks you can also drive

**Sunset on the Columbia River.**

across the Bridge of the Gods, if you choose, and return to Portland via the North Shore route. Or you can drive west, back along the 80-N Freeway.

The Bridge of the Gods is a private toll bridge, although there was once, according to Indian legend, a *real* bridge, a natural arch that spanned the river.

If you choose to return via Interstate 80-N, plan to stop at a point of interest just west of Bonneville Dam. As you approach Moffett Creek get into the left hand lane of the freeway and turn off into a small open area just after you cross the freeway bridge.

The Moffett Creek Arch is just north of the freeway. At the time this bridge was built, in the early 1900's, it was the longest 3-hinge concrete span in the world and it received national publicity for that fact. It was considered to be one of the most interesting bridges on the Old Highway.

Be careful of traffic when you walk across the freeway. You can walk down to an old road, just east and north of the freeway, to inspect the bridge.

The remainder of the trip back to Portland affords interesting views of the falls, cliffs and the great expanse of the lower Columbia River.

Fishermen along
the old canal
at Cascades Locks
(right).
Moffett Creek Arch
(below).

### Trip 3, Trail 1 • McCord Creek

**Approximate distance: 3.0 miles round trip (3.7 miles round trip including trip to lower falls)**

Take the Ainsworth Park-Scenic Highway exit from Interstate 80-N, turn left immediately on the Warrendale-Dodson road, then stay to the right or you will return to the freeway. Continue for 2.3 miles to a sign identifying Yeon State Park. This is just before the road rejoins the freeway, east-bound. The parking area is to the right just beyond the park sign.

A path leads up from the southwest corner of the parking area to an old water tank. Turn left at the tank and continue to follow the path, which plunges through a tunnel of deciduous trees. As you emerge you will see a sign "McCord Creek Falls, 1.5 miles."

The wide path now tours through a section of towering conifers, veers left and rises for a short distance to a "T" in the trail. The trail to the left leads to the base of the lower falls, a distance of 600 yards.

The trail leading right from the "T" is to the upper falls. It is well maintained, with no false trails leading from it. You will find a multitude of wildflowers in season.

Climb via switchbacks to where the trail runs along an overhanging cliff. At this point the trail is quite narrow, with an iron railing on your left to protect you from a sheer drop. You will pass high above the lower falls, with a good view down into the canyon. The trail passes the upper falls and ends at the creek edge.

McCord Creek Falls
from the Lower
McCord Creek Trail.

### Trip 3, Trail 2 • Tanner Creek Falls

**Approximate distance: 1.0 mile (1 way)**

(This trail is *not* recommended either for small children or the elderly, due to the poor condition of the trail.)

To reach the trailhead, take the Bonneville Dam exit from Interstate 80-N.

Turn right at the stop sign after the exit, then immediately right again, then immediately left. Just beyond a small parking space to the left a chain across the road restricts automobile traffic.

Step across the chain and follow the road along the east bank of Tanner Creek for 0.2 miles, when you will come to a small dam. The road ends here, but continue along the east bank of the creek. You will clamber over big rocks, past a small waterfall that sprays gently down a huge rock to your left. After you get over the rocks you will see a path leading up the left bank of the creek.

The Tanner Creek Trail can be difficult at times because it is extremely hard to maintain, due to frequent small slides, but Tanner Falls is a lonely, magnificent spot, worth the effort required to reach it.

Tanner Creek plunges into a huge cirque, then rushes out around giant boulders. Above are what appear to be solid rock walls, overgrown with moss and vegetation of various kinds, including a few small trees.

In the spring of 1973 a portion of the west wall a short distance downstream from the falls slid down and blocked the stream, creating a small, beautiful lake, which appears to be up to 30 feet in depth in some spots. Since it is not a solid dam, but one formed with rocks and trees, Tanner Creek continues to run under and through it and at this writing opinions differ whether the dam will hold and the lake remain, or whether the lake will eventually drain away.

Regardless of future events, you can lay down on one of the boulders and stare up those walls and feel that you are lost in time and space. Like certain sections of the Eagle Creek Trail, you may feel what I term the "cathedral experience." The mystic harmony of Nature is very much at work here.

Please — don't disturb it.

**Tanner Creek Falls.**

**Trip 3, Trail 3 • Wauna Viewpoint**

**Approximate distance: 1.5 miles (1 way)**

To reach the Wauna Viewpoint Trail, park in the picnic parking lot near the entrance to the Eagle Creek area and walk down the road to the suspension bridge. Just across the bridge, on the west side of Eagle Creek, turn to the right and you are on the trail. It is plainly marked at this point.

The trail has some narrow spots and many switchbacks as it rises steadily, paralleling Eagle Creek. After a turn to the west the trail now parallels the freeway (again with switchbacks). Unfortunately, because of the proximity to the freeway you are never able to entirely escape the noise of civilization.

One possible point of confusion lies ahead: about 0.7 miles from the trailhead you will come to a place where the trail switches back very sharply, while another path continues straight ahead across a small open area with moss-covered rocks both above and below. The last day I climbed to this particular point the remains of a giant, fire-scarred tree, with a broken top, marked the point where the main trail switched back. (The path ahead proceeds for about one-fifth of a mile to a circle marking the end of Tanner road.)

From this switchback the Wauna Viewpoint Trail rises steadily, but with no more false trails. This trail offers many good views of Bonneville Dam and the town of Bonneville across the Columbia River, and you will pass beneath the transmission lines from the dam.

From the viewpoint at the end of the trail you can see east far beyond the Bridge of the Gods and many miles downstream to the west.

**Bridge of the Gods and town of Cascade Locks from Wauna Point.**

**Trip 3, Trail 4 • Eagle Creek**

**Approximate distances:**
**1.5 miles (1 way) to Metlako Falls**
**2.0 miles (1 way) to The Punchbowl**
**3.5 miles (1 way) to High Bridge**

Eagle Creek! For generations of Oregonians the words will always denote an exclamation of wonder and delight.

Eagle Creek is unquestionably Nature's masterpiece in the Gorge, and the Eagle Creek Trail is man's supreme effort in trail building.

Have respect for this trail, and stay on it. In a recent summer no less than four serious accidents were reported and all could have been avoided if people had been more careful.

The trail was built in the early 1900's, leading to the discovery of the fossilized remains of flora thousands, perhaps millions of years old. Many scientists were attracted to the site to classify specimens, which included a ginkgo tree.

To reach the trailhead, drive the road along the east bank of Eagle Creek for 0.8 mile. Parking at the trailhead is rather limited, and the area will be crowded on summer week-ends, for this is one of the most heavily traveled trails in the Gorge.

The trail is narrow in spots, and care should be taken with small children. At various places a sharp and often sheer drop must be passed. When there is a perpendicular cliff to the left in these places, a hand cable is provided along the cliff.

The trail rises quickly so that you are soon above the creek and the view is breathtaking, with the sharp drop to the right and the clear blue of the water in the deeper pools visible most of the time. The trail parallels the east side of the creek to the High Bridge, and continues from there to Tunnel Falls (6.0 miles) and Wahtum Lake (13.0 miles).

At Metlako Falls, a short side trail provides a view point.

The Punchbowl is the most famous, and most photographed, of the falls on the trail. The Lower Punchbowl Trail (1.8 miles from the trailhead) leads down to the

**Many small waterfalls tumble down the steep banks of Eagle Creek.**

creek and will enable you to get a head-on view of the Punchbowl.

For a view of the Punchbowl from above, stay on the main trail to the viewpoint at 2.0 miles from the trailhead.

I recommend the trip to the High Bridge. As you approach the bridge the trail narrows and below and immediately to your right the creek rushes through a narrow fissure in the rocks.

My favorite time to walk the Eagle Creek Trail is when the mist is in the trees and the clouds hang low, forming a ceiling for what is truly a natural cathedral. A vertical rise along the west bank is heavily timbered. In the winter and spring many small waterfalls course down this bank.

Any attempt to describe the experience of being alone on the Eagle Creek Trail is but an exercise in futility, the recognition of the complete inadequacy of words.

### Trip 3, Trail 5 • Buck Point Trail No. 439

**Approximate distance: 1.0 mile (1 way)**

The Buck Point Trail originates at both the picnic area and the campground at Eagle Creek.

From the picnic area, follow the sign which reads "Buck Point Trail No. 439. Ruckel Creek Trail, ½. Buck Point 1".

The trail leads to the left above the fish ponds in the Eagle Creek hatchery, then cuts back to the right around a small ravine before it turns left again to a fence above the freeway. It then follows the fence for 120 yards before it emerges into the campground area. A sign here reads "Ruckel Creek Trail No. 405, Oregon Skyline Trail 6."

Follow around to the right, circling the campground, and you will come out just above campsites 6 and 7. A sign here reads "Buck Point Trail No. 439. Buck Point 1."

Buck Point Trail starts as a very gentle path, but it does get steeper as you progress. Still, it is not difficult.

The trail has many switchbacks and relatively few views of interest until near the end. It is, however, a pleasant walk offering some good photographic possibilities at Buck Point on a clear day.

**Along the Eagle Creek Trail.**

**Trip 3, Trail 6 • Ruckel Creek**

I list no approximate distance for the Ruckel Creek Trail because the only portion of it that I can recommend for the beginning walker is to the bridge over Ruckel Creek and a detour from there down a stretch of the remains of the Old Highway immediately beyond. So consider this a relatively short walk, but one well worth taking.

The Ruckel Creek Trail originates from the campground at Eagle Creek. A trail marker will be found at the north end of the campground near a fence above the freeway.

The trail winds down to a large open area. Cross this, bearing close to the right bank, and you will find the trail sign again.

Once up on the bank, follow along a torn up section of the Old Highway a short distance to the Ruckel Creek Bridge. There have been slides along here at various times, and part of the Old Highway is obliterated, so you may have to scramble a bit in spots.

You will find a beautiful old stone bridge, with a small waterfall dropping directly beneath it at Ruckel Creek. From here you can walk along a delightful section of the Old Highway for about 300 yards. Nature is busy with her own reclamation project here and moss, needles and new vegetation already conceal much of the hard surface of the road, while the trees have arched above it to make a shaded walkway.

If you feel inclined to tackle the Ruckel Creek Trail, climb up the east bank of the creek for about 200 yards. From there on it is quite steep and hard work, at least for these old legs. Veteran hikers will find it an enjoyable experience. Novices will make many stops to catch their breath.

**The melody created by rocks and water is an integral part of the Gorge's charm.**

# Trip 4

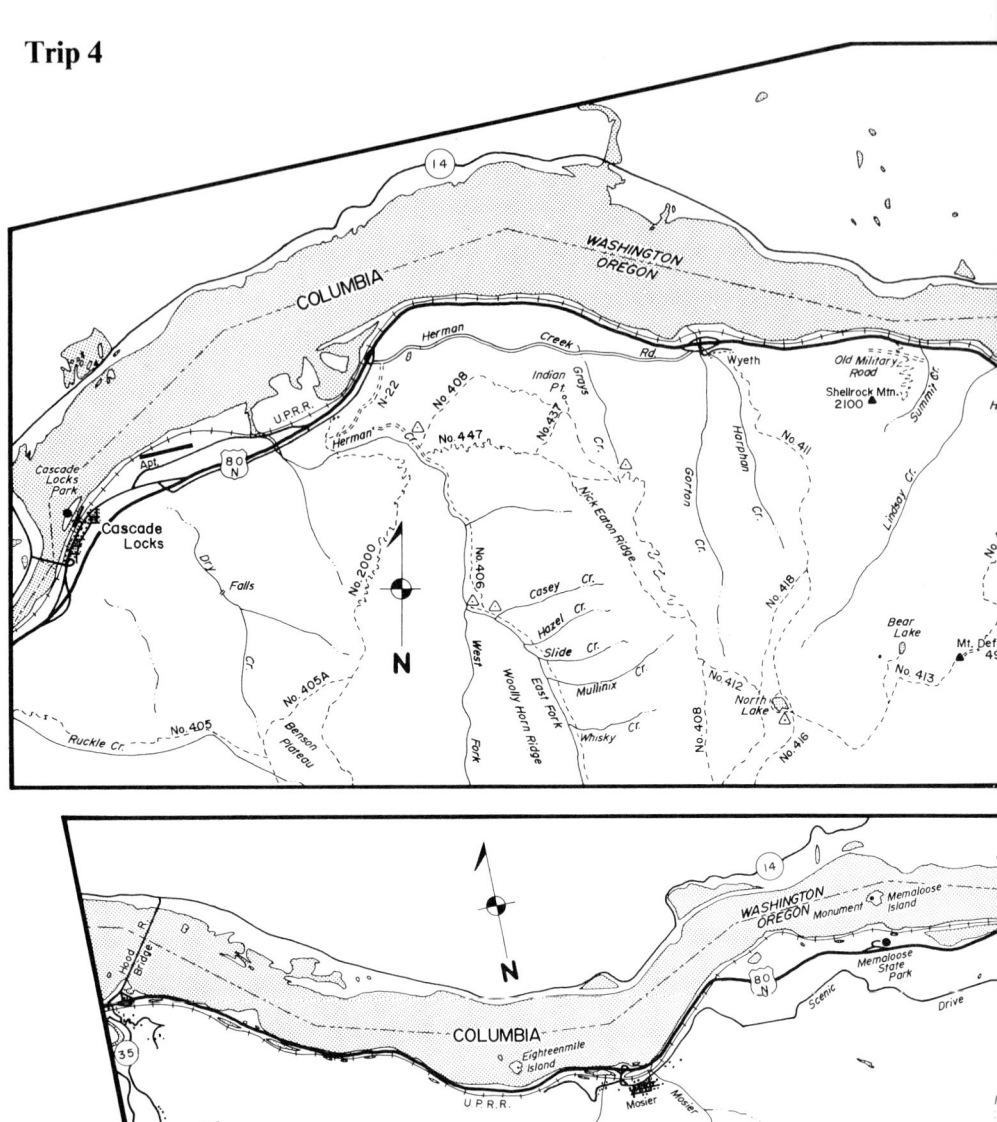

**Trip 4**  (Cont'd)

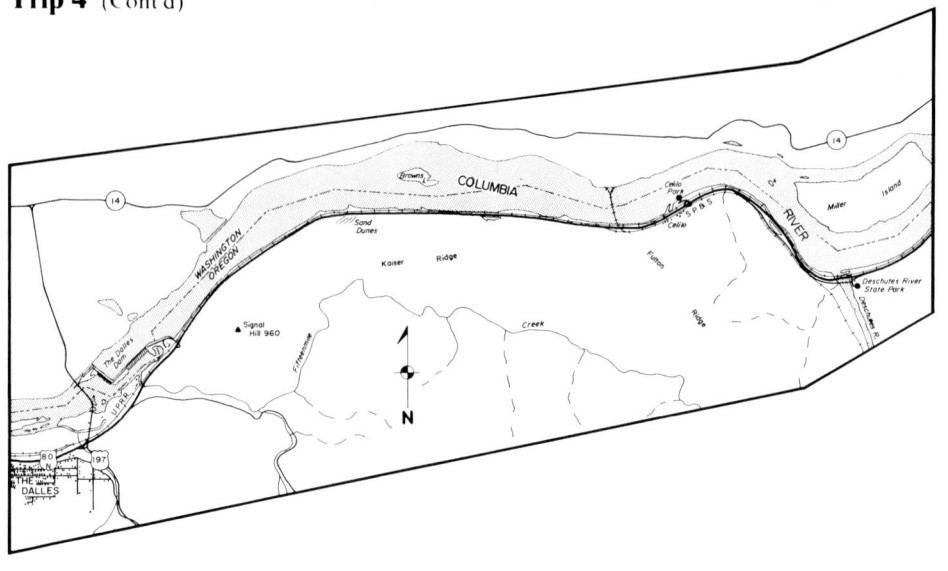

Impounded waters of the Columbia River cover all but the tip of Memaloose, "The Island of the Dead." Marker visible in this photo is monument of Victor Trevitt, who chose to be buried with the Indians on Memaloose.

# Trip 4 • Cascade Locks to Deschutes River and Return

**Points of interest:** Starvation Creek Falls, Rowena Crest, Celilo Park, Memaloose Island, Lancaster Falls.

**Picnic grounds:** Starvation Creek Falls State Park, Viento State Park, Lausman Memorial Park, Mayer State Park, Celilo Park, Memaloose State Park.

**Campgrounds:** Viento State Park, Deschutes Campground, Memaloose State Park.

**Trails:** Pacific Crest Trail loop at Herman Creek, Herman Creek Trail, Hole-in-the-Wall Falls Trail, Perham Creek-Wygant Trail.

On the map Trip 4 shows as merely an extension of Trip 3, but in experience it is totally different, as it extends from Cascade Locks, just east of the heart of the Gorge, to the arid land along the Deschutes River.

Just 11.0 miles east of Cascade Locks, a short distance after you pass a sign indicating "Starvation Creek State Park," glance out the car window to your right and you will see "Hole-in-the-Wall Falls," a waterfall that gushes out the *middle* of a cliff. (See Trip 4, Trail 3 for details.)

Starvation Creek Falls is the last of the major waterfalls in the Columbia River Gorge. There is a modern restroom near the parking lot and picnic tables along the creek itself. It is a short walk up to view the falls.

The name Starvation Creek comes from a long ago experience when a train attempted to break through the heavy snowdrifts between The Dalles and Portland. The train was trapped in a snowslide at a spot not far from the falls, and food was brought in by individuals on snowshoes (some say on skis, but this is disputed), to supplement the meager food supply the passengers carried with them.

Viento State Park, just a short distance to the east on the freeway, has a picnic area to the right of the road, and a modern campground to the left. The latter is a bit

**Starvation Creek State Park.**

close to the railroad.

Another short jog down the freeway and you will notice an exit road to the right. As of this writing there is no sign to indicate its destination, but up on the side of the hill is the Anna and Vincenz Lausman Memorial Park. It is a picnic area, as yet not fully developed.

From the parking lot there is a view across the river of an old log flume, and if you walk up the hill away from the parking lot to the right there are some interesting rock formations high up on the mountain.

At Hood River, one of the two major cities on the Oregon side of the Gorge, you can take some side trips through apple and pear orchards towards Mt. Hood. When the orchards are in bloom or when the fruit is ripe in the fall, it is a worthwhile jaunt.

Just east of Hood River the hills begin to flatten out and on the far side of the Columbia they become barren and brown in the summer, a lovely shade of pale green in the winter and spring.

Take the Scenic Highway exit at Mosier, pass through the village and begin the climb to Rowena Crest. Now you really make the transition into another world, as first you pass through a few small orchards and then, ever climbing, through scattered clumps of trees that are stunted in comparison to the gigantic firs you passed only a few miles to the west.

This is a world of cliffs and canyons, the Columbia River is out of sight for all but an instant here and there, although the sheer cliffs that lead to the river on the north shore can be seen most of the time.

Stop at Rowena Crest for a view upriver, then descend to the river level and the freeway via the Rowena Loops, a twisting, scenic drive. Near the end of this make a very sharp turn back to the left and follow the road across the freeway and railroad bridge to Mayer State Park, a picnic facility by a lagoon, where fishing, swimming and boating are available.

Return to the highway, which soon rejoins the freeway.

The Dalles is a modern city and the largest single settlement in the Gorge. It was

**The view east from Rowena Crest.**

the western terminus of the Oregon Trail. At one time the Columbia River was 200 feet (or less) wide here and an early description said that "the river turned sideways and rushed between two narrow, rockribbed walls."

Just east of The Dalles there is a monstrosity in concrete known as The Dalles Dam. This monument to the aesthetic values of the U. S. Army Corps of Engineers destroyed Celilo Falls, the great gathering place for Indians for many centuries. Celilo Falls could have been developed into possibly the major tourist attraction along the river, but now Celilo Park, a few miles upriver from the dam, is a lonely little park, frequented by seagulls and an occasional curious traveler who has been misled by highway signs indicating "Ancient Indian Fishing Grounds."

Seagull at windswept Celilo Park (left). View of flume on Washington shore from Lausman Memorial Park (below).

Take the Celilo Park exit, turn right, then immediately left, on Highway 206, and proceed along the road, paralleling the freeway, for approximately 3.0 miles to the Deschutes River.

A large campground is located on the east bank of the Deschutes, but it may be filled during the fishing season.

The Oregon Trail crossed the Deschutes at this point. Prairie schooners were floated across the river, livestock swam it, while women and children were ferried across in canoes by Indians who were paid for their labor with trade goods.

This, by our definition, is the end of the Gorge. Beyond here, to the east, the hills are low, and the freeway soon climbs to the top of the ridge and continues on through central and eastern Oregon.

Return via the freeway, and just after you pass under Rowena Crest you will see a large sign indicating "Memaloose Park."

Memaloose Island, in the Columbia River, was known as "The Island of the Dead." Memaloose, from the Chinook "Memalust," means "to die," and it was on the island that the Indians deposited their departed, wrapped in skins or blankets and placed in a sitting position, sheltered by grave houses of pole and bark. These Indian remains were removed before water rising behind Bonneville Dam innundated about 85 percent of the island.

Still visible on the island is a monument that marks the grave of Victor Trevitt, a pioneer printer who moved to The Dalles in 1854. Trevitt, a member of the first state legislature in Oregon, chose to be buried on Memaloose with the Indians.

Picnic tables and modern restrooms are located in the rest area, and a road to the west leads to a large, modern campsite.

Continue west on the freeway and just after you pass Starvation Creek Falls State Park take the time to look up on the cliff to your left. One of the most delicate waterfalls in the Gorge is best seen from this spot. The falls is unnamed, but there is a move afoot to have it named "Lancaster Falls" and we have used that terminology in this narrative.

**Fishermen on Deschutes River. Deschutes Campground in background.**

**Trip 4, Trail 1 • Herman Creek loop, via Pacific Crest Trail No. 2000 and return via road**

**Approximate distance: 2.0 miles round trip**

The Oregon section of the Pacific Crest Trail traverses the backbone of the Cascade Range for the entire length of the state. The trail, in its entirety, extends from Canada to Mexico.

The northernmost section of the trail in Oregon leads to Benson Plateau, a total distance of approximately 13.0 miles, with an elevation gain of almost 5,000 feet.

The first mile of this famous trail leads to a footbridge at Herman Creek and is a very leisurely and enjoyable walk. From the bridge the trail rises steadily for about the next 5.0 miles.

To reach the trailhead, take the Cascade Locks exit from the freeway. Proceed through Cascade Locks on the main street and follow the signs indicating airport and industrial park. This road leads to the south side of the freeway and to the junction of the Herman Creek Road. Turn left, and in a short distance you will arrive at the Columbia Gorge Work Station.

The trail begins at the west end of the work station parking lot. After about one-third mile it emerges onto a power line access road. Follow this road to the right until it begins to descend. At that point turn left where the unmarked path leads up to the left.

Continue up the trail for about 100 yards to where the trail forks. A sign indicates that the left fork will take you to Bear Spring Camp and Herman Creek Trail. Follow the trail to the right, which rises gently but steadily for about 400 yards, then levels off and descends to the bridge over Herman Creek.

After crossing the creek the trail soon begins the rise to Benson Plateau.

Return via a road you will see to the right shortly after you return across the footbridge. This is a pleasant walk up to the top of the hill. Cross the open area at the top, turn left on the unmarked footpath which leads down to the power line access road and back to the work station.

**Hiker pauses to admire the view from the Herman Creek bridge.**

### Trip 4, Trail 2 • Herman Creek Trail No. 406

**Approximate distance: 5.0 miles (1 way) to West Fork of Herman Creek if you walk in from Columbia Gorge Work Station. 3.0 miles (1 way) if you drive in to Herman Creek trailhead.**

If you want to be deep in the woods, far from the sound of traffic, then the Herman Creek Trail offers that luxury.

Depending upon Forest Service regulations at the time, you may or may not be allowed to drive in to the trailhead.

Exit from Interstate 80-N at Cascade Locks, drive through the city to the intersection with Herman Creek Road, and follow it to road N-22, which is a limited maintenance road. If there is no locked gate barring your way you can drive up this road for about 2.0 miles to the end of it, which is the beginning of the Herman Creek Trail. This road is one-way in spots, inclined to be rough, and quite rocky. If you cannot drive up it, or if you choose to walk in from the Columbia Gorge Work Station, take a right turn after you cross the freeway and return to the west, paralleling the freeway, and park in the designated area at the entrance to the Work Station.

Follow the Pacific Crest Trail, which exits from the west end of the Work Station area, to and across the powerline access road. A short distance after you cross this road a sign pointing to the left designates "Herman Creek Trail." Follow this up the hill (a bit steep), to where it emerges on to the road. From there it is 1.0 mile to the Herman Creek trailhead.

The trail starts as a continuation of the road but soon becomes a path. At about 0.4 mile, after an almost level walk, you will come to one of the most truly delightful little waterfalls in the Gorge. To my knowledge, it has no name, but it slides down a sheer cliff for about 80 or 90 feet, creating a fine showery spray, ending in a tiny pool at the base.

This section of the Herman Creek Trail has towering trees and high vertical slopes. It is an extremely interesting woodland walk. You may well see many small

animals and perhaps an owl or two along the trail.

The trail rises steadily, but it is not a strenuous walk. At 2.5 miles from the trailhead you reach the intersection with Casey Creek Way.

A few feet past the Casey Creek Way intersection a sign on a tree indicates "West Fork Herman Creek," which is another 0.5 mile to the right.

The latest indication from the Forest Service is that they do not intend to maintain this latter trail. However, it is reasonably easy to follow, if you don't mind ducking overhanging branches, and it leads down to the creek and a small, unofficial camp below a small waterfall.

**Trip 4, Trail 3 • Hole-in-the-Wall Falls**

**Approximate distance: 1.0 mile (1 way)**

Hole-in-the-Wall Falls is not the official designation, but a name attached some time ago by a Forest Service official. Since the name is descriptive of the nature of the falls, it has become accepted.

Hole-in-the-Wall Falls was created by the State Highway Department to alleviate a road hazard. The waters of Warren Creek periodically became impounded at the top of the cliff by an accumulation of loose rock during low water periods. When the rains began the water would exert enough force to flush this rock out and across the highway below.

The solution to the problem was to divert the creek by a tunnel through the cliff. A heavy iron mesh was placed at the top to hold back the loose rock.

The trail to the top (to Warren Creek) is not recommended for smaller children as there is one very narrow section with a sheer drop to the left.

The trail begins at Starvation Creek Falls State Park. Take this exit from the Interstate 80-N freeway, park in the parking lot, then walk back to the entrance road and there should be a small sign designating "Trail No. 413," just to the left of the fence along the freeway. Follow

Log near the base of "Lancaster Falls" on Trail to Mt. Defiance.

along the left side of the fence for 150 yards and you will be directly under the freeway sign that reads "Rest Area."

Continue along the fence as it begins to slant away from the freeway: Follow an old road bed, near the base of the cliffs to your left, and another 150 yards will bring you to the foot of wispy Cabin Creek Falls.

Continue along the old road bed, which gradually becomes a path that plunges into a small section of woods. This is the general area of some old bake ovens that were used originally by the Chinese cooks when the railroad was built. These bake ovens were only recently re-discovered.

About 450 yards from Cabin Creek Falls you will emerge into a meadow. There is a trail sign at this point, and you will see Hole-in-the-Wall Falls to your left, and high up to your right, Lancaster Falls.

Cross the meadow to your left (directly south) and walk across Warren Creek on the rocks. Follow the trail up the opposite bank and along the south side of Warren Creek for a few yards, then veer away to the left and ascend for almost 200 yards before the trail levels out. Just as you cross under the power line there is a sharp switchback to the left and this is Trail 413-B, Warren Creek.

Trail 413-B continues for slightly less than one-half mile to Warren Creek above the falls. As you approach the top of the cliff the trail runs right at the edge with a drop on one side. The trail then turns right and follows above the west bank of Warren Creek, gradually dropping down to the creek level.

If you were to continue on Trail No. 413, instead of taking 413-B, you would be on the trail to Mt. Defiance, a distance of about 5.0 miles with an elevation gain of 5,000 feet. Even though you might not feel like that extensive a hike, a walk up the trail some distance is worthwhile. You will come to the base of Lancaster Falls a short distance past the 413-B switchback, and another one-third mile beyond that the trail forks, with the right path being the original first section of the Mt. Defiance Trail. It has since been relocated to begin at Starvation Creek Park. This trail will bring you back to the freeway, some distance west of the park, in the vicinity of Lindsay Creek.

**Trip 4, Trail 4 • Perham Creek-Wygant**

**Approximate distance: 3.5 miles (1 way)**

One of the lesser-known trails in the Gorge is the Perham Creek-Wygant Trail. The trailhead is just 2.0 miles east of the exit to Viento State Park. At this point the freeway crosses a very small creek. If you are heading east there is parking space to the right of the freeway, along the fence.

A section of an old roadbed runs along the edge of the woods and then along the base of a cliff to the right. Climb the fence, walk down to the old roadbed and use it to cross the creek. Continue along the roadbed and you will soon see some evidence that this was once a picnic area. Walk to the base of the cliff and turn left, entering the woods along a pair of tracks

This old ladder was once an integral part of the Mt. Defiance Trail. The trail now bypasses the ladder which is located just above the powerline road a few hundred feet above the freeway.

that soon dwindle down to a path.

The trail continues up the west side of Perham Creek for about one-third mile, then it rises above the creek and switches back to the right. The trail continues to rise as it leads back another one-half mile to an opening affording an excellent view up and downriver.

The trail then veers left, away from the river, and after a short distance through the woods it intersects a powerline access road. Cross the road and continue up the trail on the opposite side. The trail again turns left, under the powerlines, for another one-fifth mile, where it veers right. At this point a red-lettered wooden sign tacked to a small tree indicates "Wygant Trail."

This trail climbs steadily but gently, switching back and forth and allowing several excellent views of the river.

Two false trails, a short distance apart, lead straight ahead, while the main trail switches back.

The best view of the river and the north shore is at a point 2.5 miles from the trailhead. Here you are far above the freeway and there really is no point in going any farther, except for the exercise, as you are not going to get a better view. The trail ends with a small pile of rocks slightly more than a mile farther on.

This is a particularly good spring trail, because of the multitude of wildflowers and many flowering dogwood trees.

---

The 18 walks listed in the foregoing section are not intended as a complete trail guide to the Oregon side of the Columbia River Gorge.

It is possible for a person to spend many days, even weeks, hiking and backpacking on trails in and above the Gorge. What has been presented in this book are those relatively short walks that will take no more than a few hours of your time.

If you are interested in more arduous climbs, or backpacking in for an overnight trip, detailed information can be obtained from the books on the recommended reading list on page 128, or from the Mt. Hood National Forest Headquarters in Portland, Oregon.

View west from the Perham Creek-Wygant Trail.

# THE WASHINGTON EXPERIENCE

The Washington experience is the view experience. From the top of Beacon Rock, a pastoral scene; from Maryhill, romantic, windswept desolation; from Red Mountain the truly awesome triumvirate of Mt. St. Helens, Mt. Rainier and Mt. Adams, the great snow-covered monarchs that tower over their lesser cousins.

Oregon's Mt. Hood is conspicuous from Washington State Highway 14 and from the trailhead to Big Huckleberry. Some other views are distressing, like the checkerboard of clear cuts in the Gifford Pinchot National Forest and the superabundance of roads in the same area. One begins to wonder at the "National Forest" designation and to question the frequently posted policy of "multiple use."

Sometimes the logging trucks press close behind you as you come down from the heights on the hard-surfaced roads. Sometimes you come around a turn on a gravel road to see these rolling behemoths bearing down on you. The drivers are good drivers, but they aren't slow. Be on the lookout, and drive with care.

In the high country of the southern Washington Cascades it seems a pity that anyone has to be in a hurry. Park your car at the head of any of the innumerable dead end roads and walk in. All of the roads lead to clear cuts. These are, after all, logging roads.

In the fall the clear cuts blaze with color as new growth struggles to erase the scar of man's transgressions.

Around a bend, a fawn totters across the road. The doe strolls protectively nearby. Stand perfectly still as the fawn lunges into the underbrush and the doe gives you a long, careful scrutiny before she follows.

Different legends abound in this country. The legend of Big Foot, the shaggy, mysterious monster who has been reported to roam in the Mt. St. Helens-Mt. Adams area; the legend of Whehatpolitan, of Beacon Rock; and the Goose Lake footprint, supposedly left there when a

View from the top of Beacon Rock includes fertile land along the Washington side of the Columbia, Bonneville Dam, and the Oregon side of the Columbia River Gorge.

pretty Indian girl leaped off the top of a mountain while fleeing an unwanted lover. (The footprint is still there, visible when the lake is very low. The legend adds that when the berry picking season is over the maid can be seen sitting on a rock near the lake, combing her hair.)

At the Indian Race Track (Trip 6, Trail 1) you can still see the depressions in the ground where the Indians gathered at berry picking time to celebrate the harvest with games, including betting on the speed of their horses and the skill of the riders. Fact, not legend. And farther north is Indian Heaven, where the Indians still have exclusive rights to the huckleberry crop in some areas.

Trip 7 circles the Big Lava Bed. Avoid the temptation to explore inside it. It is tricky country at best.

On both the Big Lava Bed Loop and the Wind River Loop you will find marshy meadows where streams are born to gurgle and splash down the mountainsides and eventually into the main rivers— the Wind River and the Little White Salmon River — and thence into the Columbia.

Unfortunately, some of the trails are open to two-wheeled vehicular traffic, and the roar of motor bikes is a sacrilege.

This is, for the most part, open, park-like country, a fragile ecological system that demands a balance. That balance is endangered. Preservation requires letters and voices raised in protest against the current desecration. Make your views known to Forest Service officials and to politicians.

The north side of the Columbia is sparsely populated and easy prey for developers.

The gift of the mighty river, the Gorge which it carved, is not for Oregonians alone. If one side is devastated, the other side suffers. If the highlands are scraped bare it is the nation that is wounded.

All of this land has historical significance, dating far back beyond the days when the white settlers first intruded. The heritage of the Gorge, the river, and the high country is an asset that can not be bought or sold. It can only be preserved — or destroyed.

**Mt. St. Helens rises above the clear cuts in this view from Observation Peak.**

# Trip 5

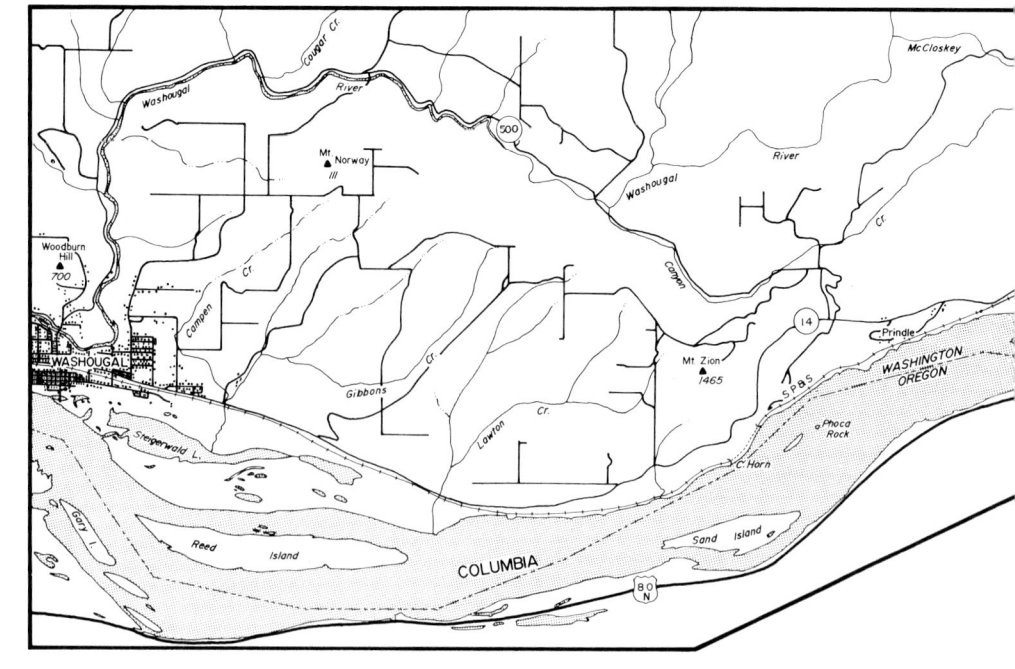

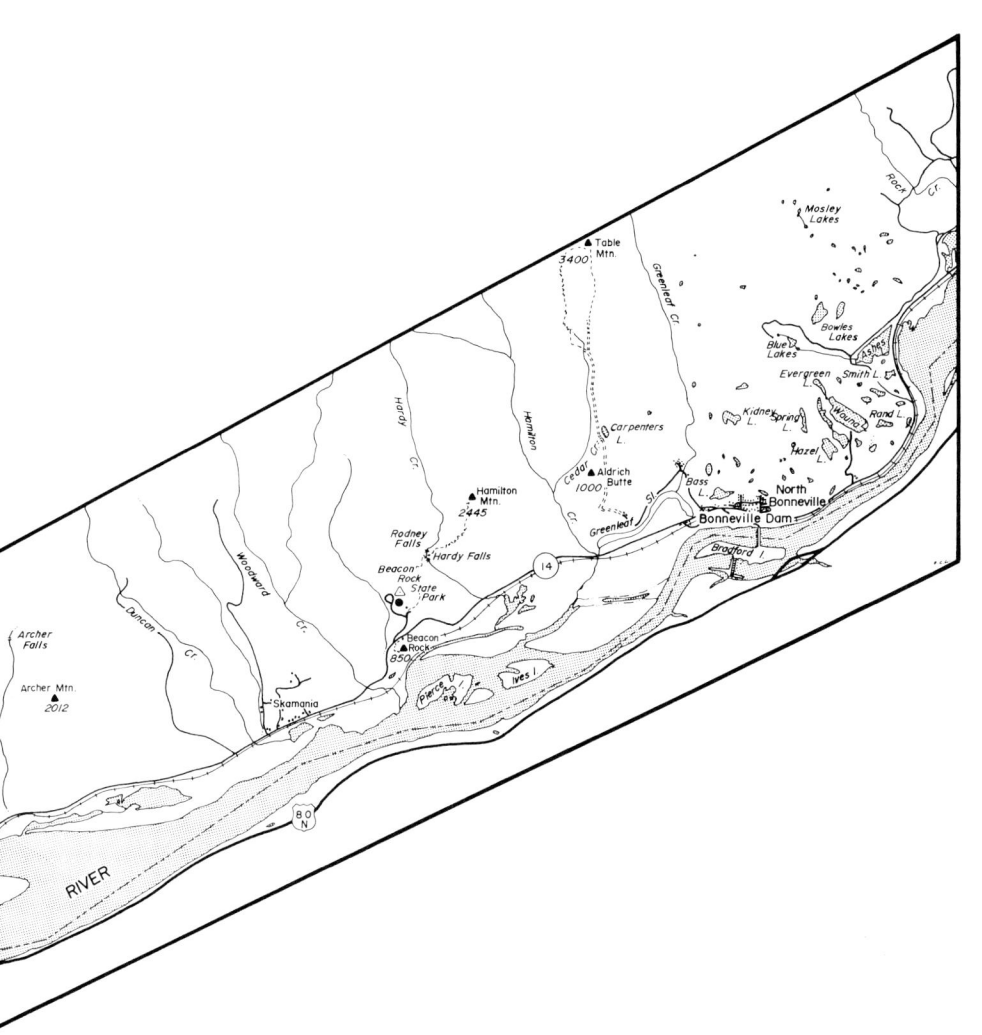

# Trip 5 (Cont'd)

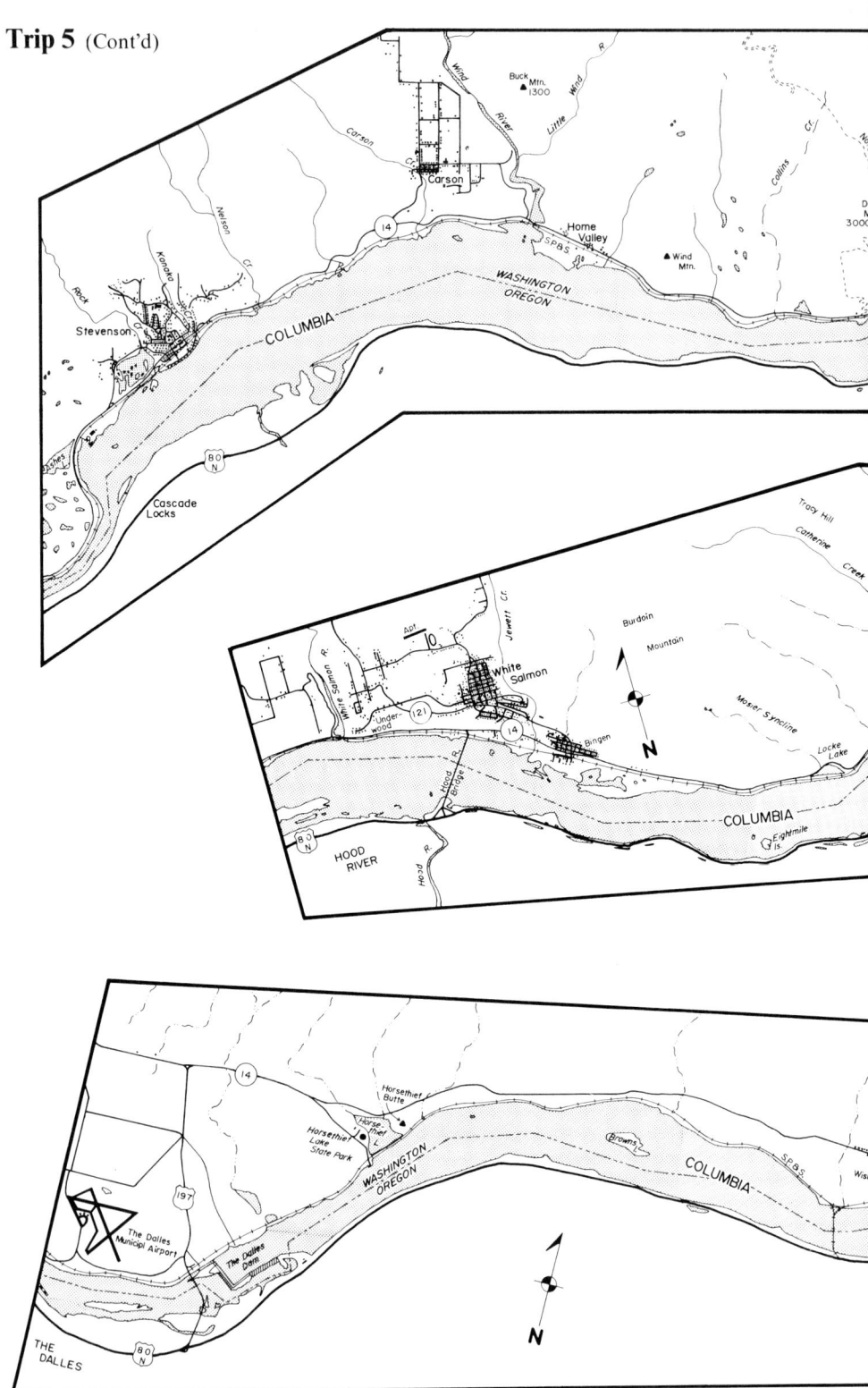

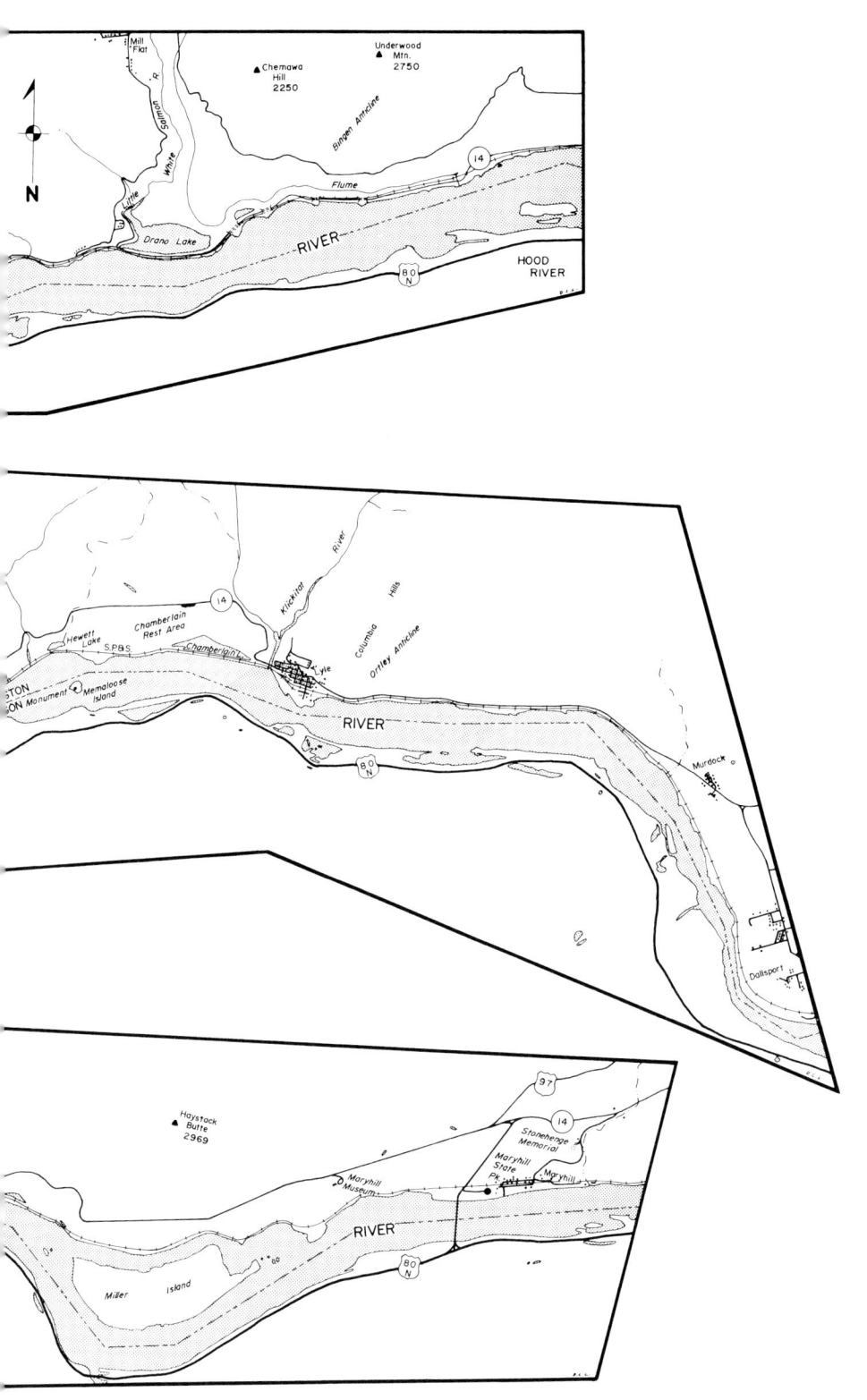

# Trip 5 • The North Shore

**Points of interest:** Beacon Rock, Chamberlain Rest Area, Horsethief State Park, Maryhill Museum, Stonehenge.

**Picnic grounds:** Beacon Rock State Park, Chamberlain Rest Area, Horsethief State Park, Maryhill State Park.

**Campgrounds:** Beacon Rock State Park, Horsethief State Park, Maryhill State Park.

**Trails:** Beacon Rock, Rodney Falls-Hardy Falls.

Washington State Highway 14 parallels the Columbia River east from Vancouver, Washington. This is a four-lane highway until just after you pass the Camas exit, then it narrows to two lanes, turns and passes through the small city of Washougal. Except for an occasional third lane for passing it remains a two-lane road the remainder of the way.

The distance from the north end of the Interstate Bridge (Vancouver) to the Skamania County line is 23.0 miles. All of the distances hereafter marked in brackets ( ) are measured from the north end of that bridge.

This trip provides interesting views of the broad lower Columbia before you reach the Skamania County border and on a clear day Mt. Hood appears to rise right at the end of the highway.

Hopefully, the state of Washington will not attempt too many improvements on Highway 14, as it is an extremely scenic route, and those individuals who are in a hurry can always cross over to Oregon and the 80-N freeway.

For purposes of definition, and lacking any clear geographic demarcation, we use the Skamania County line as the western terminus of the Gorge in Washington. A large green sign marks the entry into Skamania County.

At this point the highway runs along the side of a bluff well above the Columbia River and for the next five miles you will get several good upriver views. The road then weaves its way to river level before it reaches Beacon Rock (37.0).

Beacon Rock has a boat moorage on the Columbia, modern restroom facilities, and, across the highway, both picnic and campground facilities.

For several miles east of Beacon Rock there are towering cliffs well above and to your left. Many persons believe that if a *real* Bridge of the Gods did exist it was created when some upheaval sheared off the southern side of these mountains.

The north entrance to Bonneville Dam (41.0) affords only a limited view of the dam. The hamlet of North Bonneville is just east of the dam exit. North Bonneville's existence is limited to the next few years, or until additional power house facilities are built for the dam. The town will then either disappear or be re-located.

Stevenson (46.0) is the county seat of Skamania County. From there east to Bingen (69.0) the road hugs the river (and the railroad tracks).

For part of this stretch short, steep cliffs block any view to the left. However, just after you cross the Little White Salmon River you can see the flume (mentioned in Trip 4) and you will see it again several times in the next few miles. The road also passes through a series of tunnels in this stretch.

Bingen is the dividing line between the east and west portions of the Gorge. The

**Indian pictograph – "She Who Watches" – at Horsethief State Park.**

hills begin to slope away from the highway east of Bingen and vegetation becomes sparse. Then the cliffs crowd down to the edge of the road for several miles.

The Chamberlain Rest Area (76.0) provides sweeping views upriver and downriver. The area is fenced along the top of steep cliffs which drop down to the water.

You can take a very short walk along a paved path out to two view points. The walk then curves down and back to the parking lot. In the winter a tiny waterfall is visible across the road. The stream then runs through a culvert under the road, along the fence at the edge of the area and over the cliff to fall into the river.

Just east of the hamlet of Lyle (78.0) the road passes through two tunnels. Beyond these the road begins to rise above the Columbia.

Now you are directly across the river from The Dalles. This is empty country, barren, raked by winds, cold in the winter, blazing hot in summer.

It is worth your while to take the exit to

**Maryhill Museum.**

Horsethief State Park (88.0). Ancient Indian petroglyphs can be studied here. Parking spaces will accommodate 100 cars and you'll find a picnic area and modern restroom facilities. A boat ramp and overnight camping areas have also been provided.

Just east of Horsethief State Park, high on a bluff above the river, there is a sign that reads:

## SPEARFISH

"Among the rocks and rapids of the nearby Columbia River early-day Indians secured an annual supply of salmon, using crude spears and nets. The salmon were smoked on rocks over a heavy bed of coals, then packed in leaf-lined baskets for winter use. Remains of Indian "pit houses" and many Indian artifacts have been discovered in this area by archaeologists. The Lewis and Clark expedition found several hundred Indians fishing here in 1805, as they had for centuries."

A few miles farther down the road, just east of Wishram Heights, another his-

**Stonehenge replica.**

torical marker sits on the bluff above the town of Wishram. It states that the word Wishram comes from the Indian "Whiscom or Wish-Ham," and that the town on the river below, across from Celilo Park, was originally called Fall Bridge.

Wishram may have been one of the most ancient Indian settlements on the North American continent. "Originally called Fall Bridge," indeed!

Maryhill Museum (100.0), was founded by Samuel Hill and dedicated by Queen Marie of Rumania on November 3, 1926. In the desolate countryside, its gardens are a green oasis.

To reach Maryhill State Park take the Highway 97 exit east of the museum and follow it down towards the Sam Hill toll bridge over the Columbia. Just before you reach the toll gates take the exit road to your left.

The park has a large picnic area with modern restrooms, shelter houses with stoves, a small beach with roped-off swimming area and just east of that, a boat ramp. Many campsites are in the campground area.

To the east, on a bluff, you will see Stonehenge, a memorial honoring Klickitat County war dead. It was erected by Samuel Hill and dedicated July 4, 1918. It purports to be an exact reproduction of the original Stonehenge on Salisbury Plains, England. Hopefully, the original is not so defaced with the scrawls of the ignorant.

You can reach Stonehenge by driving east on the road in front of Maryhill State Park. Turn left when you see the "Dead End" road sign and follow the road up the hill. A road exits to Stonehenge, a few miles east of Maryhill Museum on Highway 14, also.

Now, if you have the time, drive back on the Washington side rather than crossing over to the freeway in Oregon. You will get different perspectives, new views of Mt. Hood — and one cannot capture the flavor of the north shore in a single trip or by driving it only one way. As with all good things in the Gorge, it demands a more leisurely perusal.

**Aerial view of Beacon Rock.**

## Trip 5, Trail 1 • Beacon Rock

No distance listed, for this is a climb up the monolith that is reported to be the world's second largest (after Gibraltar).

The base of Beacon Rock covers 17 acres and it rises to a height of nearly 900 feet. It stands between Washington State Highway 14 and the Columbia River 37 miles east of Vancouver.

The trail up Beacon Rock was started in October, 1915, by Henry J. Biddle, assisted by Charles Johnson, and completed in April, 1918. The climb is neither as dangerous nor as difficult as it may at first appear.

Follow the signs and you will soon begin climbing up the monolith with the aid of metal handrails and catwalks. The first part of the trail is up the southwest face, then it switches to the southeast side and just before you reach the top, back to the west face. Thus you are offered a variety of views as you climb.

At the top the guardrail ends. A few steps take you up to the flat top of the rock. Be careful if you decide to take these last few steps, for to the east is a sheer drop.

Beacon Rock occupies a unique spot in the history of the Gorge. Indians tell about a princess by the name of Whehatpolitan, who climbed the rock with her baby to escape from her angry father. Unable to get back down, she and the child perished on top of the rock, and it is said that their wails can still be heard along the Columbia River.

Henry J. Biddle, of Portland, purchased the rock to prevent it from being quarried. Upon his death ownership fell to Erskine Wood and other Biddle heirs.

In 1931 the U.S. Army Engineers were building jetties at the mouth of the Columbia River and the subject of quarrying the rock arose again. The heirs had offered Beacon Rock to the state of Washington as a gift, but it had been rejected on the grounds that it was an evasion so the owners would not have to pay taxes on it.

At this point Sam Boardman, parks engineer for the Oregon State Parks Commission, conceived the idea of having the state of Oregon accept the rock as a gift and creating an Oregon State Park in the state of Washington.

In a letter to J. C. Ainsworth, president of the U. S. National Bank of Portland, Boardman wrote: "I believe that this historical landmark should have the guardianship of a sovereign state. Washington refused its acceptance. Oregon can ill afford to leave it to the whims of commercialism."

In his reply, Ainsworth stated that he had contacted Erskine Wood, who said he would consider giving a deed to the property to the state of Oregon for one dollar. Ainsworth requested that Boardman check to see if the state of Oregon could legally acquire the property.

Oregon and Washington newspapers began to pick up the story. Washington state papers were particularly upset at Oregon officials for what they termed "overstepping recreational boundaries."

The resulting uproar caused the state of Washington to create Beacon Rock State Park.

Boardman wrote: "With all this stirring of recreational interests, home pride rekindled through the effrontery of a bordering state . . . the rock is saved to posterity. While not under the jurisdiction of Oregon it is ours to see and wonder at its birth."

Thus ended the episode of the "S. O. S. Wehatpolitan," as Boardman whimsically termed the effort to preserve the scenic landmark.

**Short section of the trail up Beacon Rock.**

**Trip 5, Trail 2 • Rodney Falls-Hardy Falls**

**Approximate distance: 1.0 mile (1 way)**

Exit from Washington State Highway 14 to Beacon Rock State Park, and follow the paved road past the picnic area to the campground site. The trailhead is at the east side of the campground.

For about the first one-fifth mile the trail is more or less under the powerline. You will pass by two powerline standards, at the second of which the trail veers left and contours along the side of a ridge, then crosses two small wooden footbridges a short distance apart.

Just beyond the second bridge there are two short trails to the right. Each leads to a viewpoint overlooking Rodney Falls. The lower of the two trails leads to the top of Hardy Falls.

The main trail continues to the base of Rodney Falls with the trail switching back to your right to cross a footbridge at the base of the falls.

Another trail goes straight ahead at the switchback, and leads to the cataract where the water plunges into a pool, then rushes out through a narrow slit in the rocks to continue its drop. Improbable legend says that the bowl-like pool was used by the Indians as a bathtub. Considering the temperature of the water it was a very cold shower.

If you elect to take the side trip to this point, take care of small children as the rocks are slippery.

The footbridge is at the base of Rodney Falls, with Hardy Falls immediately below it. The trail goes up the opposite bank and a side trail soon leads to the right.

Follow this trail down to the creek and you will be just above Hardy Falls.

From the footbridge the main trail continues to the top of Hamilton Mountain, a distance of about 3.0 miles. This is a steep trail, with 72 switchbacks. An exhausting climb, but the first part of it is worth taking, as at the top of the first series of switchbacks a side trail off to the right affords a fine view of the Gorge.

Tangle of logging roads in Gifford Pinchot National Forest. For map showing route of Trips 6 and 7 please see overleaf.

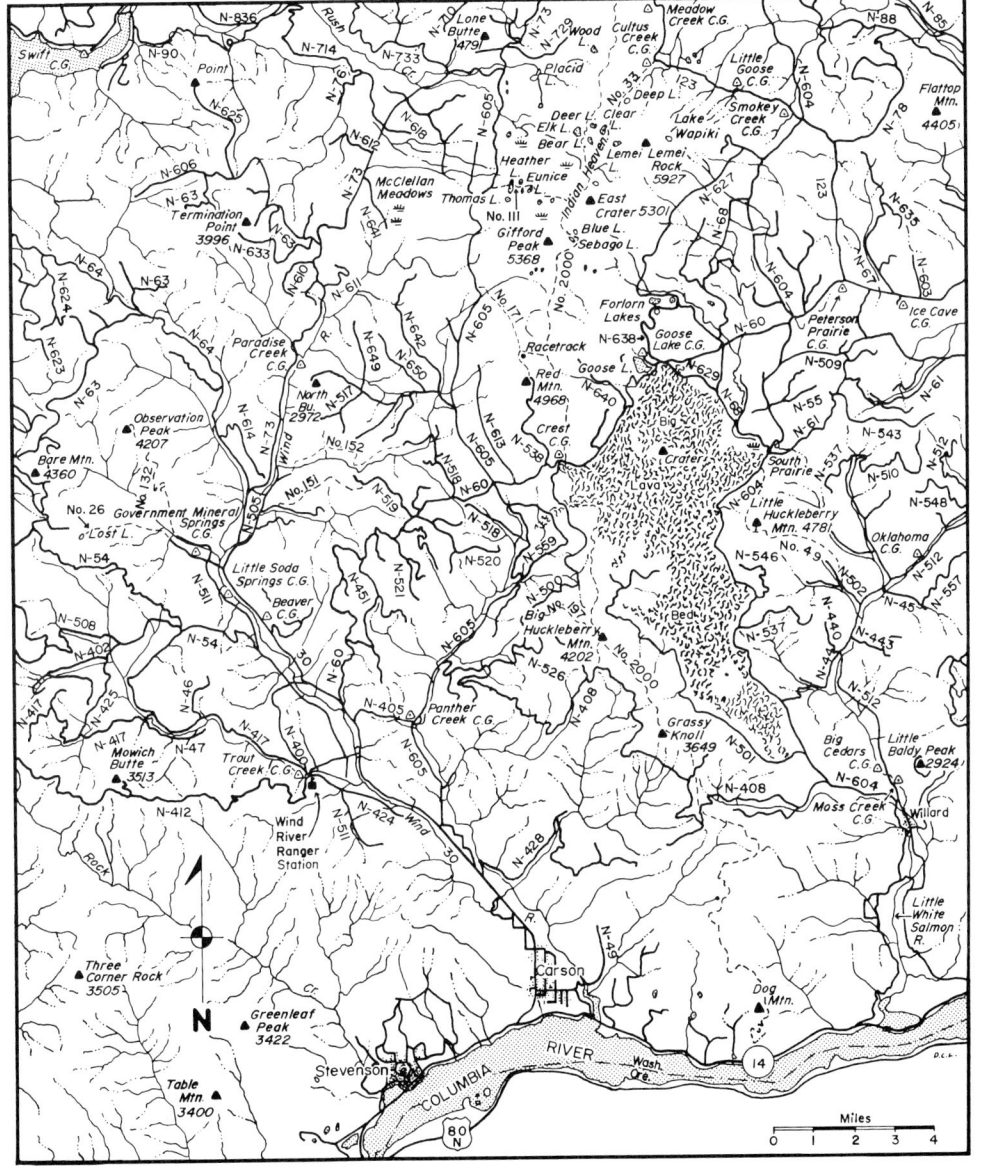

**Trips 6 and 7**

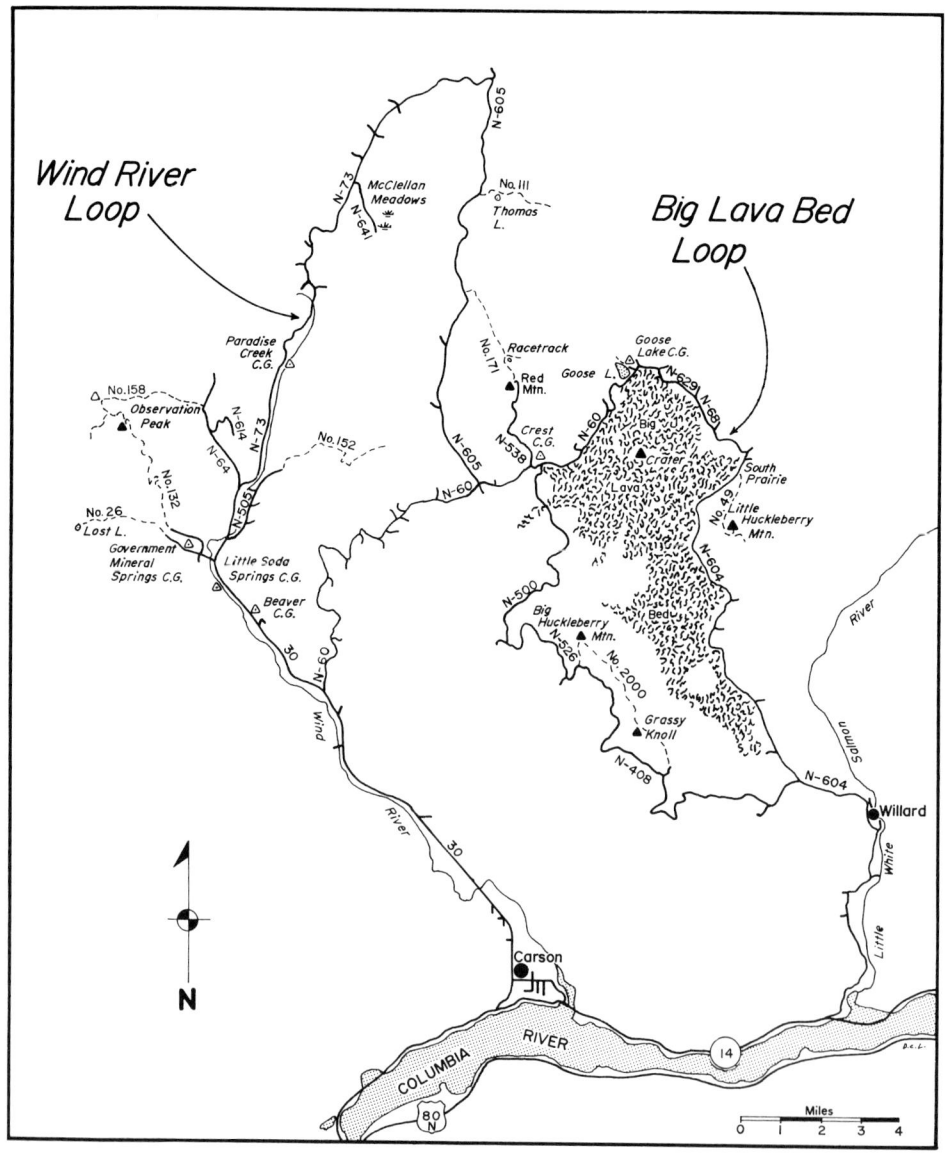

## Trip 6 • Wind River Loop

**Points of Interest:** "Iron Mike" and "Big Mike" Mineral Springs at Government Mineral Springs Campground.

**Campsites:** Paradise Creek, Government Mineral Springs, Little Soda Springs, Beaver, Trout Creek.

**Trails:** Indian Race Track Trail, Red Mountain, Thomas Lake Trail, McClellan Meadows, Lost Lake, Falls Creek.

Excellent views of beautiful snow-capped mountains, the possibility of seeing deer along the road, and the promise of sensational fall colors are some of the benefits that await you on this trip.

Take the Carson exit 49 miles east of the Interstate Bridge on Highway 14. Follow the paved road north through the hamlet of Carson and then continue in a northwesterly direction. About 3.5 miles after you leave Highway 14 you will cross the Wind River. This is a level road bridge, but if you pull over to the side and walk to the center of the bridge you will see that the river has cut a very deep canyon.

Many side roads lead from the road you are traveling, but stay on the main road for approximately 9.5 miles to Road N-60, which exits to the right. The sign there indicates Trout Lake 31, Red Mtn. 16, Goose Lake 18.

Road N-60 is a narrow road, asphalt for about the first 8 miles, then a good gravel surface. The road winds and climbs steadily and many short, dead end service roads take off from it. You may want to drive or walk down some of these. Walking is recommended, because it will give you a chance to be alone in the forest area.

Always stay on the roads or the trails, however, as it is easy to get lost. In spots the forest is quite dense.

As you continue along the road you will begin to catch glimpses of Mt. St. Helens. If you succumb to the urge to photograph here, save film for the better views ahead.

Approximately 22.0 miles on Road N-60 brings you to the intersection with Road

N-605. The sign here indicates that it is 11.0 miles to Road N-73. Turn left on N-605 and continue.

(If the weather is ideal for photography and you want to get some excellent shots, here is a recommended side trip. This entails *not* exiting onto N-605, but continuing on N-60 to the intersection with N-538, about 3.0 miles farther on. This is an unimproved road, but you can make it up to the lookout on Red Mountain for a sweeping view).

After you make the left turn on N-605, Mt. St. Helens will loom larger and larger and there are several excellent spots to stop for photographs. About 5.0 miles after the turn you will arrive at the trail head to Indian Race Track Trail No. 171. Absolutely the best view of Mt. St. Helens on the regular loop trip is obtained at the trailhead to Thomas Lake, a few miles farther down the road.

You will intersect with Road N-73 at about 35.0 miles, and in a few miles it will become hard surfaced and take you back to Carson and thence to Highway 14 in a relatively short time.

You can easily drive this entire loop, taking time for some short stops, in about 3 hours. You should figure one hour each way to the highway exit from either Portland or Vancouver, which still leaves ample time for some of the walks included in the trail descriptions.

## Trip 6, Trail 1 • Race Track Trail No. 171

### 2.0 miles (1 way). Continue to Red Mountain Lookout, 1.5 miles (1 way)

The trailhead is 27.0 miles from the exit from Highway 14. A small parking space will be found on the right hand side of the road about 50 yards before you get to the trail sign. You can follow the path out of the parking space and pick up the regular trail in the woods without difficulty.

This walk starts out level and remains so until you cross the small creek which is the only water available along the trail. If you have canteens, fill up here.

On the other side of the creek, the trail rises up and away from it. Although there

**Aerial view of Indian Race Track**

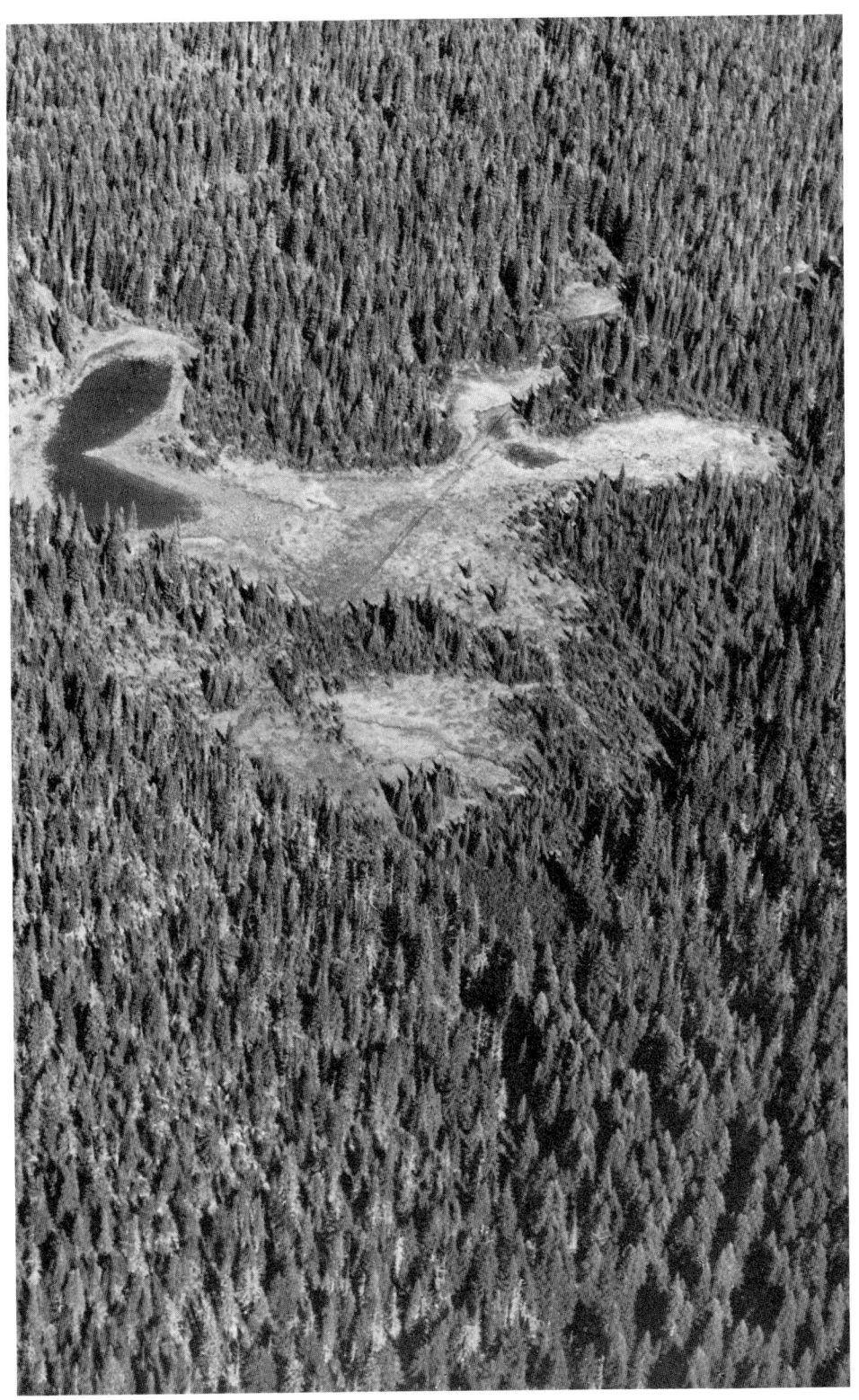

are a few relatively sharp rises, the trail for about the next mile is not exhausting. The last mile is an almost level walk.

Horses are allowed on the trail, but motorized vehicles are banned. The trail is well-defined and there are no false trails leading from it. After passing a small, marshy meadow to your left the trail drops slightly and then opens into a larger meadow area. There may be a shallow lake here through the spring and early summer.

Beyond that is a larger meadow where the Indians used to gamble and race their horses at berry picking time. Since the races were last run some forty years ago it is not easy to spot the track from this level. It is much easier to see the track from the climb above to Red Mountain. The track is usually visible from certain spots on your way up to the Lookout in the late afternoon. However, that is a very steep trail. The trailhead to Red Mountain is on the southwest side of the large meadow.

**Trip 6, Trail 2 • Thomas Lake**

**Total distance: slightly less than 1.0 mile (1 way)**

One of the easiest and most delightful little walks in this book is the trip in to Thomas Lake, a few miles north of the Race Track Trail on N-605.

The trailhead sign is on the left hand side of the road and ample parking space will be found on the right hand side where the trail begins. The only excuse for missing the trail is the truly breathless view of Mt. St. Helens to the west.

This is an almost level walk through parklike surroundings. At 0.6 mile you will see a small lake on your left, and almost immediately thereafter you will glimpse Thomas Lake through the trees to your right. In the first lake complex there are three — Heather Lake, Thomas Lake and the small one for which I found no name. Backpackers use a campground at the north end of Thomas Lake.

Also at the north end is a footbridge, and if you cross and walk on for a short distance you will come to Eunice Lake,

**Fog on Thomas Lake.**

where the trail apparently ends.

For an interesting little side trip to an alpine meadow, take the trail that branches up the hill to your right shortly after you cross the footbridge at Thomas Lake. This rises sharply for a short distance, then emerges into the meadow. The trail continues across the meadow and into the woods where it eventually intersects with the Pacific Crest Trail. This latter trail will lead you to Indian Heaven.

**Trip 6, Trail 3 • McClellan Meadows**

**Approximate distance: 1.8 miles (1 way)**

There are two entries to the McClellan Meadows Trail No. 150, one from N-605 and one from N-73. The trail connects these two roads. I recommend the west entry, from N-73. Take the N-641 dead end exit road and drive in approximately 1.0 mile to the end of the road. Parking is available for three or four cars. In the course of this drive you have passed the meadows, a large and occasionally boggy area where elk and deer sometimes feed.

From the road end, continue down the tracks of the old road and into the woods. The tracks soon narrow down to a trail.

Although the Forest Service doesn't rate any kudos for the way the immediate area has been handled, it is still a pleasant walk. The luxuriance of ferns and other ground cover, the presence of small streams, plus the large bird population, make up for the desecration at either end of the trail.

It is 1.8 miles to N-642, another dead end service road. You might as well turn around here becuase the remainder of the route to N-605 crosses clear cuts and isn't at all interesting.

**Bird nest near trail.**

### Trip 6, Trail 4 • Lost Lake
### Approximate distance: 3.5 miles (1 way)

This is probably the most difficult walk in this book. Prepare accordingly, for there is quite an elevation gain.

To reach the trailhead, drive to Government Mineral Springs Campground, which is 1.0 mile west of N-73, just northwest of the Carson Fish Hatchery. A large sign makes the exit to the campground easy to spot.

Drive through the campground and take the exit road at the far end indicating "summer homes." At the end of this road there is a circular parking area. Hike along the old road tracks on from there and you will soon be on the trail. It is approximately one-third mile to the creek crossing, and this is the last water until you reach the lake itself.

Shortly after you cross the creek the trail begins a steady rise, switching back and forth across the ridge, which narrows as you near the top. While there are no really impressive views along the trail, you will experience a marvelous sense of solitude if you pause to rest often, as I did.

Lost Lake itself is a small jewel, tucked away at an elevation of more than 3,700 feet. There is room for campsites where the trail ends, as well as at other spots around the lake.

Leopard Lily.

**Trip 6, Trail 5 • Observation Peak**

**Approximate distance:**
**6.0 miles (1 way) via Observation Peak Trail No. 132**
**4.0 miles (1 way) via Trail No. 158**

You can make a one-day round-trip of this walk if you start on trail No. 132 and then walk out on trail No. 158. To do this, however, requies having a car and a driver willing to pick you up at the second trailhead, as they are some distance apart.

The trailhead for No. 132 is at Government Mineral Springs Campground, near the summer homes area. The trail commences at the bridge over Trapper Creek, and proceeds up Trapper Creek, contouring in and out of several side canyons. At about the 5-mile point the only switchback turns sharply left and continues for 0.5 miles to the summit of the peak. Originally there was a lookout cabin here in the form of a groundhouse which was burned several years ago. The grade up to the peak is relatively gentle.

From the summit you can see Mt. St. Helens, Mt. Rainier and Mt. Adams, as well as the Goat Rocks and a myriad of lesser peaks including Red Mountain. The view to the south extends no farther than the peaks above Lost Lake.

Although the peak looks like a cinder cone from the east it is timbered all the way to the summit on the south and west.

Along trail No. 132 you will find some very attractive wooded areas as well as vast huckleberry fields.

To reach the trailhead for trail No. 158 continue on N-73 past the Government Mineral Springs Campground junction and exit to the left on Road N-64. Just after you pass the exit to Road N-614 (to your right) you will make a right hand turn on N-64. The day I made this trip a cardboard sign was tacked to a post on the left hand side of the road with the inscription "Conditional Survey Trail 158 MP." A wide shoulder on the road offers ample parking space.

This trail has many low, overhanging branches as well as several logs fallen

*Observation Peak Trail No. 132 begins at foot bridge over Trapper Creek.*

across it, but it is easy to follow. From the road the trail winds down to Hollow Creek, which can be forded easily except in times of very high water, and then begins a steady rise for about one-half mile. After that it levels out in stretches, with some short rises.

At about 1.5 miles you will begin to hear a creek off to your right, and in the next one-half mile you will get a glimpse of a waterfall in the trees to the right of the trail. At 2.0 miles you will reach a tiny creek in a small, open area. From there the trail leads up to the intersection with Trail No. 132 and you can continue on to the summit of Observation Peak.

**Trip 6, Trail 6 • Falls Creek**

**Approximate distance:**
**3.0 miles (1 way) to campsite at falls**
**4.6 miles (1 way) total distance**

Classify this as an intermediate walk —and one of the more enjoyable ones.

The trailhead is at the end of road N-505. This is a dead-end road, which exits from N-73 just north of the N-64 exit.

N-505 is a gravel road (also known as Washout Road) that climbs up to the right of N-73 and then parallels it. About one-half mile after you start on N-505, Sheep

Road exits to the right. A marker at this point indicates Trail No. 152 straight ahead. Watch for these trail markers for the rest of the trip.

Nine-Mile Creek is 1.0 mile from N-73 exit, and just beyond that N-505 becomes a dirt road to the left on the fork. A sign at this junction indicates Falls Creek Trail No. 152. Follow the dirt road for another mile to Falls Creek. Two side roads exit along the way, but at each junction the Trail No. 152 sign is quite prominent.

When you come to a "Y," take the right fork, then pull into parking area beside sign at the trailhead. The trail leads up the right side of the creek for about 200 feet, then crosses to the left via a footbridge.

Just a few yards after you cross the bridge you will come to an old logging road. Follow this road to the right, and you will soon locate the trail. At about one-half mile the trail begins a gentle rise up the left bank of the creek, then veers off to the left through the woods and continues in a fairly gentle ascent for approximately another 1.5 miles.

You are always within sound of the creek, although sometimes it fades to a gentle murmur. At 2.0 miles the trail rises quite sharply for almost one-half mile up the far left bank of the canyon. Then it levels out and you can continue to a primitive campsite on the creek bank. A small waterfall enhances this altogether lovely spot.

You can continue on from here — a level walk all the way — for almost another mile during which you are both out of sight and sound of the creek. Then you will hear a gentle, gurgling noise, and discover the creek immediately to your right. A short distance farther you will come to a large, marshy meadow which appears to be the origin of Falls Creek. The trail tours around the edge of this meadow and shortly thereafter emerges onto an old logging road. From there it is about one-fifth mile to the opposite trailhead.

You can, of course, reverse this procedure by making the entrance from this end, but I recommend the three-mile walk in from N-505.

**Falls Creek from camp site on creek bank.**

## Trip 7 • Big Lava Bed Loop

**Points of interest:** Willard National Fish Hatchery, Goose Lake.

**Campgrounds:** Goose Lake, Crest Campground.

**Trails:** Goose Lake Lakeshore Trail, Big Huckleberry, Grassy Knoll, Little Huckleberry.

The Big Lava Bed Loop trip begins approximately 58 miles east of the Interstate Bridge. Exit from Washington Highway 14 at the sign on the left that reads "U.S. Fish Hatchery & Nutrition Lab., Willard."

The road climbs up and away from the Columbia River, paralleling the west side of Little White Salmon River, although the latter is not visible from the road. It is approximately 3.5 miles to the hamlet of Mill Flat. At the "T" follow the sign which designates "Willard."

Just after you pass through Willard you will cross Lava Creek and immediately thereafter will see a road to the left and a sign, "South Prairie 13, Goose Lake 18." This is Forest Service Road N-604.

After about four miles on N-604 you will begin to see evidence of lava beds on your left, and they will be much in evidence during your trip to Goose Lake. The forest is reclaiming much of the lava bed, but it still has a ways to go.

The hard-surfaced road ends about five miles from the beginning of N-604, but the remainder of the trip to Goose Lake is on a good gravel road. As you approach the South Prairie Junction you will see a beautiful meadow to your left. At the junction you turn left on road N-68.

Watch for additional junctions along the way, and follow the signs indicating Goose Lake. According to my map you are on N-629 for a short distance, then on N-60. However, the road signs were not clearly indicated the last time I took the trip.

Goose Lake is a small lake at the northwest edge of the Big Lava Bed. White, barkless trees rise like mournful ghosts from the water, quite close to the road. The

**South Prairie.**

Forest Service campground has a boat ramp, several campsites, picnic tables, and outdoor privies.

To continue the loop trip go south on N-60. You will rise to about 3,500 feet, but the gravel road is usually in good condition. Crest Camp, is of course, near the crest of the road. It is a Forest Service campground with tent sites and NO WATER.

Shortly after you pass Crest Campground road N-500 exits to the left, and the sign there indicates "Road N-408, 7 miles." You can take this cut-off or continue on N-60 to the intersection with N-605. (The latter road runs down the east side of Panther Creek, although well above it, and intersects with N-408 in a few miles.)

If you got a late start, you can continue on N-605 and come out on the road to Carson, and thence back to Highway 14. However, the road back over the crest, via N-408, offers spectacular vistas as well as to the trailhead of two main hikes, Big Huckleberry and Grassy Knoll. N-408 is a twisty, gravel road, but well maintained.

A word of caution: driving on gravel requires some special techniques, rather different than the highways or streets most of us are used to traveling. If you stay within the posted speed limits, usually 25 mph or 35 mph, you shouldn't experience difficulty. If you exceed the limits or if you slam on your brakes, you could be in trouble. Cars slide easily on gravel and the edge of the road is close to some sharp drops on N-408.

Also remember that there may be logging trucks along the road, so drive with care. No thrill quite like looking up to see one of those bearing down on you as you round the curve on the wrong side of the fairly narrow road.

Along with the vistas, the view from N-408 also offers some unfortunate examples of over-zealous clear cutting.

Several roads intersect N-408, and again, they are not always well marked. However, the signs indicating WILLARD *are* easy to spot, and if you follow them you will eventually rejoin N-604, a short

**Goose Lake.**

distance from Willard and Mill Flat.

This is an easy one-day trip from Portland or Vancouver, and a reasonably early start will allow you to take at least one of the walks, descriptions of which are to be found in the following pages.

Late September or early October is a good time for Trip 7, for the vine maple and big leaf maple are extremely colorful about that time of the year.

**Trip 7, Trail 1 • Goose Lake Lakeshore**

**Approximate distance: 1.0 mile (round trip)**

This delightful little walk begins at the far end of the loop road leading through the campground at Goose Lake.

The trailhead is well marked, and the trail leads down to the waters edge, then continues towards the end of the lake. Ecologically, this is one of the more interesting trails in this book, as it runs to the shallow end of the lake, then along the marsh where the lake begins to form and thence up along the creek.

The last 250 yards are rather steep, and the trail ends at the base of a small waterfall. A very short side trail leads to creekside, about 175 yards below the waterfall.

**Trip 7, Trail 2 • Big Huckleberry Trail No. 186**

**Approximate distance: 3.5 miles (1 way)**

No water is available on this trail. Also, the trailhead is in open country, but the trail leads through some fairly deep forest and has some rise to it – and this combination can create a considerable temperature change, so dress accordingly.

Ample parking will be found at the trailhead on N-408 and a very large sign indicating the trail, so locating it is not difficult. There is a great view of both Mt. St. Helens and Mt. Hood from the trailhead.

The trail rises immediately, well above the road, and then parallels the road for

Swimmer in Goose Lake.

about one-third mile before it turns left and leads into the woods. It contours along the side of the ridge for about another one-half mile, then turns right and begins to rise to the top of the ridge, approximately another one-fifth mile.

The trail then continues along the crest of the ridge, generally rather level but with a few short rises. There is one small, open area about 2.0 miles from the trail head, but you will emerge into a much larger area at about 3.5 miles, where you can see Mt. Hood soaring skyward to the south, rising high above the walls of the Gorge and the brief stretch of the river that is visible from this point.

You can continue indefinitely, as the trail intersects with the *Cascade Crest Trail* at 4.0 miles, but for a simple afternoon walk of three or four hours duration this is a good place to stop, take some pictures, have a snack and return to your car at the trailhead.

### Trip 7, Trail 3 • Grassy Knoll

**Approximate distance: 2.0 miles (1 way)**

The trailhead is at the junction of N-408 and N-408-D, the latter a dead end road. A sign identifies the trail, "Crest Trail 2000, Grassy Knoll 2."

There is no water on the trail, and there is some rise, so a canteen is advised.

The trail starts across an open area that is literally carpeted with wildflowers in the spring. You will see flowers all along the way as the trail enters the woods and then goes up the series of rises that bring you, eventually, to the round ridge top known as Grassy Knoll.

The scanty remains of an old lookout are on the top, and the area immediately surrounding the remains is littered with broken glass.

Although the latter part of the trail looks quite steep when you view it from the nearest vantage point, it is really not difficult to climb and you get a "top of the world" feeling when you reach the broad, open spaces at the top.

Pond at South Prairie.

Mt. Adams
from Grassy Knoll
(left).
Benchmark on the
summit of
Little Huckleberry Mountain
(below).

## Trip 7, Trail 4 • Little Huckleberry
### Approximate distance: 2.5 miles (1 way)

The trailhead to Little Huckleberry Mountain is 20.4 miles from the turnoff from Highway 14 — or approximately one-half mile south of the intersection of road N-604 and N-68. Although the trailhead is not marked, it is located where an old side road leads off to the southeast.

The first 200 yards is an almost level grade, then a short, steep climb of 100 feet. Then curve right and climb a steady, rather steep grade along the crest of a slope. After about one-third mile the grade moderates as it traverses above a small ravine, then the grade increases considerably as it climbs a narrow ridge crest.

Just after you pass the one-mile marker the trail levels out, then begins to drop downhill for the next one-third mile, when it begins to climb again. You will cross a small stream that does not flow all season, and also pass a camp area where the water supply comes from a pipe and also does not continue all season.

There are a few switchbacks until you reach the two-mile mark, then the trail traverses north along the western slope at a moderate grade for the next one-quarter mile. At this point the trail leaves the woods.

Watch for a fork in the trail. The main trail is level for a short distance and then drops to the southeast along a ridge crest where it eventually meets Road N-502 near the Little White Salmon River.

To reach the summit of Little Huckleberry Mountain, take the left branch and begin climbing along the open slope of very low ground cover consisting of grass, flat bushes and a few widely scattered, low evergreen trees.

When you come to a faint fork in the trail, keep right and continue uphill. The trail soon forks again and you can take either one, as they soon rejoin, and at that point you can see the rock foundation of the lookout that once stood on the summit. Another one-tenth mile climb will take you to the top.

The trails in the Gifford Pinchot National Forest that are listed in this book are but a minute fraction of the hundreds of miles of trails available for your exploration in the Southern Washington Cascades.

For other books showing additional trails please refer to the recommended reading list below, or get maps and additional information from the various National Forest Headquarters or local ranger stations.

Other books you may find to be of interest include:

Hiking the Oregon Skyline

Wildflowers 1, The Cascades
(The Touchstone Press)

Trips and Trails, 2

102 Hikes in the Alpine Lakes, South Cascades, and Olympics
(The Mountaineers)

Cover Photo:
High Bridge, Eagle Creek Trail

Editor:
Thomas K. Worcester